THE THREE MUSKETEERS

NOTES

including
- *Life of the Author*
- *Introduction to the Novel*
- *List of Characters*
- *Brief Plot Synopsis*
- *Selected Genealogies*
- *Summaries & Comme⸱*
- The Three Musketee⸱
- *Suggested Essay Questi⸱*
- *Selected Bibliography*

by
James L. Roberts, Ph.D.
Department of English
University of Nebraska

INCORPORATED
LINCOLN, NEBRASKA 68501

Editor

Gary Carey, M.A.
University of Colorado

Consulting Editor

James L. Roberts, Ph.D.
Department of English
University of Nebraska

ISBN 0-8220-1300-2
© Copyright 1989
by
Cliffs Notes, Inc.
All Rights Reserved
Printed in U.S.A.

1999 Printing

Cliffs Notes, Inc.   Lincoln, Nebraska

CONTENTS

THE THREE MUSKETEERS
Notes

LIFE OF THE AUTHOR

Alexandre Dumas was perhaps the most popular author of the nineteenth century, and his best works continue to be popular today. Two of his novels, *The Three Musketeers* and *The Count of Monte Cristo*, are ranked among the best adventure stories of the world and have been read by countless thousands. *The Three Musketeers* has also been the subject of many movies and has inspired many similar types of swashbuckling films.

Born on July 24, 1802, Dumas was one of the most prolific writers of the nineteenth century. His father, a mulatto, was somewhat of an adventurer-soldier and was not a favorite of Napoleon because of his staunch republicanism. When his father died, young Dumas was only four, and the family was left in rather severe financial straits. The young boy's formal education was scanty, most of it provided by a priest, and as soon as he could qualify, Dumas worked in the office of a lawyer. As he grew older, he became close friends with the son of an exiled Swedish nobleman, and the two of them began to dabble in vaudeville enterprises.

As a young man, Dumas went to Paris and secured a position as a clerk to the Duc d'Orleans; this was a marvelous stroke of good fortune, for the Duc would soon become king, and Dumas would write a superb memoir about his many and varied mishaps while he was employed by the future king. At the same time, Dumas and an old friend, Adolphe de Leuven, produced several melodramas.

When Dumas was twenty-two, his life underwent a drastic change: first, he wrote and produced his own melodrama which was a popular success and, second, he became the father of an illegitimate son by a dressmaker. When the boy was seven, Dumas went to court to get custody of the boy and succeeded.

Professionally, these years were extremely happy times for Dumas; for six years, he and Leuven had been collaborating on plays, and their legitimate dramas had been staged to much popular acclaim. In 1829, Dumas' *Henry III et sa Cour* (Henry III and his Court) was produced; it was Dumas' first spectacular triumph. The Duc was so fond of it that he appointed Dumas the librarian of the Palais Royale.

The Revolution of 1830 interrupted Dumas' playwriting, and for a pleasant and amusing account of these years, one should consult Dumas' memoirs for many richly humorous anecdotes (don't worry unduly about the degree of truth in them). Later, because Dumas was implicated in some "irregularities" during a noted general's funeral, he decided to "tour" Switzerland; as a result, we have another long series of memoirs, this time issued as travel books. It should be noted, though, that Dumas always retained his affectionate relationship with the Duc and that he eventually returned to France, where he composed many first-rate, long-running plays.

Dumas' well-known collaboration with Auguste Maquet began in 1837 and resulted in a series of historical novels in which Dumas hoped to reconstruct the major events of French history. For example, in *The Three Musketeers,* the musketeers are united in order to defend the honor of Anne of Austria (the queen of France) against Cardinal Richelieu's schemes. This particular novel was so popular that Dumas immediately composed two sequels and, by coincidence, his other great novel, *The Count of Monte Cristo,* was also written during this same creative period, even though the time periods of the two novels vary greatly.

With the aid of collaborators, Dumas turned out so much fiction and miscellaneous writing that it has been remarked that "no one has ever read the whole of Dumas, not even himself." We know now, however, that Dumas' assistants provided him with only rough plot-lines and suggested incidents. He himself filled in the outlines, and all of his manuscripts are in his handwriting.

Like so many creative and productive men, Dumas' life ended in a series of personal and financial tragedies. He built a strangely beautiful and impressive French Gothic, English Renaissance hybrid mansion and filled it with a multitude of scavenger-friends; both his home and his hangers-on were tremendous drains on his purse, as was the construction and upkeep of his own theater, the Theatre Historique, built specifically for the performance of his own plays.

In 1851, Dumas moved to Brussels, as much for his political advantage as to escape creditors—despite the 1,200 volumes which bore his name—and he died not long after a scandalous liaison with an American circus girl, a situation that he might well have chosen as a fictional framework for his demise.

Dumas' son, Alexandre ("Dumas *fils*"), is remembered today chiefly for his first novel, *The Lady of the Camellias,* which was the basis for the libretto of Verdi's opera *La Traviata,* as well as the plot of one of Hollywood's classic films, *Camille,* starring Greta Garbo.

INTRODUCTION TO THE NOVEL

In order to understand and enjoy this novel to the fullest, one should be acquainted with a special kind of novel—the "swashbuckling novel," a novel which is filled to the brim with intrigue, adventure, and romance. One rarely, if ever, encounters this kind of novel in contemporary fiction, and it was very popular during the nineteenth century. Dumas was a master of this genre.

Basically, the swashbuckling novel combines the best elements of the novel of intrigue, the novel of adventure, and the novel of romance. The novel of intrigue involves plots and sub-plots in which one person or a group of people are involved in elaborate plots or schemes of one nature or another. This kind of novel is often, but need not be, about love and is frequently concerned with the intrigues of spies, the takeover of some enterprise, or political intrigue.

The novel of adventure is, as the term suggests, one which involves all kinds of adventures, most commonly those which take place on the highroads. For example, d'Artagnan's trip to London to retrieve the diamond tags for the queen and his various adventures and encounters with the enemy along the way constitute a novel of adventure. Usually, a main character's life is at stake, but this need not be necessarily so.

The novel of romance involves a simple love story of some nature, and there are several basic love stories in *The Three Musketeers*—for example, the duke of Buckingham's love for Anne of Austria, the queen of France; he will do anything for the pleasure of being in her presence. D'Artagnan is continually astonished at the duke's extravagant sacrifices – merely to please this lady. Likewise, d'Artagnan will undertake a dangerous journey solely because of his love for and devotion to Constance Bonacieux, a love that is, as we see toward the end of the novel, deeply reciprocated.

The term "swashbuckling" refers most often to a combination of the above three elements, accompanied by extreme histrionics – fantastic dueling and hair-raising escapades, narrow escapes, and desperate situations. These escapades are often seen as heroics – such as the episode where d'Artagnan and the three musketeers make a bet to stay in the bastion for an hour, and during this time, they stave off a number of the enemy.

Most often, the term "swashbuckling" is associated with dueling, especially when the hero is outnumbered by lesser swordsmen or when he encounters a superb opponent and yet easily disarms or conquers him. There is a good deal of swaggering (especially by Porthos); there is also a good amount of bantering, bragging, bravado, and exaggeration (by all three of the musketeers and d'Artagnan), and, of course, d'Artagnan is the perfect example of the swashbuckler because he is handsome, an expert dueler, and a superb swordsman. D'Artagnan is a young man captivated by love and romance and willing to undertake any type of adventure merely for the sake of adventure – but certainly for the sake of the woman he loves.

LIST OF CHARACTERS

D'Artagnan (dȧr·tȧn yän')

The main character of the novel, d'Artagnan was raised in the French province of Gascony, an area known for its courageous and brave men. The novel begins with his departure from home and his arrival in Paris, taking with him virtually nothing but his good looks, his honesty and integrity, his loyalty to both the king and the cardinal, and his expert swordsmanship. Despite initial blunders and difficulties, d'Artagnan quickly makes friends with the three musketeers, and later he finds himself in a position to do a great service for the queen of France. D'Artagnan's name has become synonymous with a fearless adventurer and a swashbuckling swordsman. At the end of the novel, d'Artagnan's dream of becoming a member of the King's Musketeers is fulfilled, and he is given a commission in the company.

THE THREE MUSKETEERS

Athos (à·tôs')

Wounded when d'Artagnan first meets him, Athos will later prove to be the person who wrote his memoirs about these adventurers. He is the most aristocratic of the three musketeers and also the oldest, but d'Artagnan feels closer to Athos than to the other two. Long before Athos reveals that he is the young nobleman who married the wicked Milady (Lady de Winter) during his youth, d'Artagnan is deeply impressed by him. Athos' real name is Count de La Fère.

Aramis (à·rà·mē')

He is supposedly passing his time as a musketeer until the queen provides France with an heir, at which time Aramis will enter the priesthood. He was brought up in a monastery, and it was assumed that he would become a priest, but when he was nineteen, he met a young lady and became extremely devoted to her. An officer ordered him never to speak to her again, and so Aramis left the monastery, took fencing lessons for a year, and eventually challenged and killed the haughty officer. Even though we are never told so directly, the lady in question is apparently Madame de Chevreuse, a close friend to the queen. She now lives in exile in Tours.

Porthos (pôr·tôs')

The most worldly of the three musketeers, Porthos is extremely proud of his worldly good looks and his fine physique, which he shows off to its best advantage by dressing to impress the women of society, who seem to fully appreciate his good looks and his courtly attentions. He is devoted to good food and comfortable surroundings. At the end of the novel, Porthos gives up musketeering in order to marry an older woman who has inherited a fortune.

THE MUSKETEERS' SERVANTS

Planchet (plän·shā')

D'Artagnan's servant. He is ultimately the sharpest of the servants and serves his master well on many dangerous occasions. Unlike d'Artagnan, Planchet is prudent, but still exhibits moments of great courage and ingenuity. Planchet is able to make a long and dangerous trip to England by himself, and at the end of the novel, he is rewarded for his daring and made a sergeant in the guards.

Grimaud (grē·mō′)

Athos' servant. Because his master is mannerly and rather reticent, Grimaud is also rather reserved. One of the comic incidents in the novel focuses on Athos' forbidding Grimaud to speak unless it is an absolute emergency. A dignified silence passes between them, and thus Grimaud upholds the quiet nobility of his master.

Bazin

Aramis' servant. Because Aramis is planning to enter the priesthood, it is only fitting that Bazin should also contemplate a future devoted to the religious life. His utmost desire is to be the servant of a high church official. Bazin believes that Aramis is capable of attaining the rank of cardinal.

Mousqueton (müs·kə·tōn′)

Porthos' servant. Like his master, Mousqueton is the most knowledgeable about worldly things. For example, when his master is wounded and is confined to an inn with no money, Mousqueton is able to poach some choice wild game and fish, and he is extremely clever about Western-style roping, a talent he puts to good use when his master needs wine. Cunningly, Mousqueton lassos bottles of wine like an expert and hauls them back to Porthos.

OTHER CENTRAL CHARACTERS

Monsieur de Tréville (də trə·vēl′)

The captain of the King's Musketeers, he is an old friend of d'Artagnan's father; thus he will be a special protector of the youthful and impulsive d'Artagnan. He also acts as d'Artagnan's special confidant and advisor and, being genuinely fond of the young man, he watches over him carefully.

Monsieur Bonacieux (bô·nän·syoe′)

D'Artagnan's unprincipled landlord who seeks d'Artagnan's help when his young wife is kidnapped; later, he becomes one of the cardinal's toadies, and he even assists in the kidnapping of his own wife.

Constance Bonacieux (kōn·stäns′ bô·nän·syoe′)

Bonacieux's wife; she is more than thirty years younger than her husband. Through the influence of her godfather, she has become the queen's linen maid; she is fiercely loyal to the queen. When d'Artagnan first rescues her from the clutches of the cardinal's men, he falls madly in love with her. Consequently, she is able to convince him to go to London in order to save the queen's reputation. Constance eventually realizes that she is in love with d'Artagnan.

Milady, alias Lady de Winter

She represents the quintessence of evil in the novel; she is d'Artagnan's wicked nemesis (someone bent on revenge). At first, d'Artagnan is deeply attracted to her physical beauty and charm; however, even after he hears how much she despises him and how she plans to have him murdered, he is still captivated by her loveliness. She acts as the cardinal's personal spy and is responsible for the deaths of (1) a young priest; (2) the duke of Buckingham; (3) de Winter's assistant, John Felton; (4) Constance Bonacieux; and (5) she is probably responsible for her husband, de Winter's, death. In all probability, she is responsible for the deaths of many other innocent, insignificant people who got in the way of her crafty machinations. Milady is finally tracked down by d'Artagnan, the three musketeers, and her brother-in-law, and she is tried and beheaded for her numerous and brutal crimes.

Lord de Winter

Lady de Winter's brother-in-law; he suspects that Milady killed his brother in order to inherit vast family properties. When she arrives in England, he knows of her intent to murder Buckingham and himself, so he has her imprisoned. After Felton helps free her and Buckingham is murdered, de Winter joins the others who are determined to punish her. He accuses her of the deaths of his brother, of Buckingham and John Felton, and he votes for her beheading.

King Louis XIII

The king of France – but not a very strong or effective king. He resents Cardinal Richelieu, but he recognizes his dependence on this powerful man.

Queen Anne, or Anne of Austria

The king's Spanish queen; she is romantically involved with the duke of Buckingham, a powerful politician in England. Since France is at war with England, Buckingham is an enemy of France; nonetheless, Anne is in love with him, and it is her intrigue with Buckingham which causes d'Artagnan to go on his first adventure to London to retrieve a gift that the queen made to the duke. Despite her love for the masterful Buckingham, Anne is faithful and loyal to her husband, the weak and incapable king of France.

Cardinal Richelieu (rē shə·lyoe')

Historically, he was one of the most powerful diplomats of his time, controlling both individual people and nations with his clever and astute machinations. In this novel, he is presented as the antagonist to the queen – primarily, we are led to believe, because she rejected his romantic advances. Richelieu has spies throughout the country, constantly monitoring the activities of the musketeers, yet he clearly respects their bravery and courage – especially d'Artagnan's, to whom he offers a commission, a lieutenancy.

George Villiers, duke of Buckingham

Next to the king of England, he is the most powerful man in England; just as the cardinal controls France, so the duke controls England. These two powerful men once vied for the love of Queen Anne, but since the duke won, he has been an enemy to the cardinal – in matters of politics *and* love. Buckingham is reputed to be the most handsome man in Europe, besides being one of the most powerful and wealthy, and he is willing to use all of his power, wealth, and influence simply to be near the queen. His love for Anne is so great that he would make any compromise for her. The cardinal knows about this devotion and uses it to his advantage. Buckingham is killed by John Felton, a puritan fanatic.

John Felton

A neurotic puritan whom Milady is able to manipulate by pretending to be a "persecuted puritan." Felton's blind devotion to his religion renders him impossible to judge the greatness of Buckingham or to look upon Buckingham as anything but a libertine who should be put to death. Felton is Milady's instrument whereby she can bring about the duke's death.

"The Man from Meung" (Count de Rochefort) (də rôsh·fôr')

This man, the personal representative of the cardinal, is also d'Artagnan's nemesis. He is the man who steals d'Artagnan's introduction to Tréville while d'Artagnan is on his way to Paris, and it is de Rochefort who continually appears at various places at unexpected times. He is the man who is twice in charge of abducting Constance Bonacieux, and he is the man who finally tries to arrest d'Artagnan for the cardinal, who ultimately orders the two men to become friends.

MINOR CHARACTERS

Bernajoux

One of the most gifted swordsmen in the cardinal's guards. He insults d'Artagnan at a tennis game, and during the ensuing duel, he is defeated by d'Artagnan, thereby making d'Artagnan's name known throughout Paris.

Count de Wardes

He first appears as a man with permission to cross the English channel when the ports have been closed by the cardinal's order. D'Artagnan wounds de Wardes, and later, in Paris, d'Artagnan discovers through Milady's maid, Kitty, that Milady is in love with the count. D'Artagnan then poses as the count in order to make love to Milady.

The Executioner of Lille

Athos discovers this man in his laboratory, piecing together a human skeleton. He shows him the piece of paper which the cardinal once gave to Milady, authorizing its bearer to demand any request. When Athos returns with the executioner, the man is wearing a mask and a large red cloak.

During the "trial scene," the executioner reveals that Milady seduced his fifteen-year-old brother into stealing church relics. Both were caught, but Milady escaped, and the boy was convicted as a common criminal; thus the executioner of Lille had to burn the fleur-de-lis onto the shoulder of his own young brother—all because of Milady's evil power. The executioner vowed to find Milady and brand her—and eventually he found her and branded her. Afterward, the brother escaped, hoping to find Milady, and the executioner had to serve out his brother's prison term. Meanwhile, Milady seduced the lord of the province (Athos; de La Fère) and spurned the runaway priest. Dejected, the young man surrendered to the authorities, and during his first evening in jail, he hanged himself.

Monsieur de La Porte

The queen's gentleman-in-waiting; he is also Constance Bonacieux's godfather. Because of his influence, Constance becomes the queen's linen maid.

Kitty

Milady's lovely and attractive maid who is infatuated with d'Artagnan and, consequently, helps him get revenge against Milady.

Chancellor Seguier

The man whom the king assigns to search the queen's room and her person, believing that she has written a love letter to the duke of Buckingham.

Monsieur des Essarts

The captain of the king's guards and d'Artagnan's superior, who urges d'Artagnan to volunteer for important missions.

Madame Coquenard

Porthos' mistress; she is about fifty – very rich and very miserly. Porthos uses his good looks and charm to get her to buy him equipment for the siege of La Rochelle.

Brisemont

Milady's hired assassin who fails in his attempt to kill d'Artagnan, but because his life is spared, he becomes d'Artagnan's devoted servant until he accidentally tastes the poisoned wine sent by Milady and dies, thus saving d'Artagnan's life.

The Queen's Ladies-in-Waiting

- Madame de Chevreuse has been exiled to Tours because the king thinks that she is conspiring against him; she is Aramis' beloved.
- Madame de Lannoy is one of the cardinal's spies; she reports all of the queen's activities to him; in this way, the cardinal knows about the diamond tags which the queen gave to Buckingham.
- Madame Bois-Tracy is a trusted friend of the queen.

BRIEF PLOT SYNOPSIS

D'Artagnan, a poor but noble young man from Gascony, leaves his home to make his fortune in Paris; he is carrying a letter of introduction to his father's friend, Monsieur de Tréville, captain of the King's Musketeers. On the way to Paris, d'Artagnan's impulsive nature gets him into trouble; he is beaten and the letter of introduction is taken from him. In Paris, he nevertheless is granted an interview with Monsieur de Tréville and is promised acceptance in the Royal Academy free of charge, where he can learn fencing, riding, and good manners; later, with experience, d'Artagnan can expect to become a musketeer.

While Tréville is writing a new letter of introduction, d'Artagnan glances out the window and, by accident, sees the person who robbed him. He runs after him, and while pursuing him, he offends three musketeers: first, he collides with Athos, reinjuring Athos' wounded shoulder; then he jostles Porthos and reveals a partly counterfeit golden shoulder belt that he is wearing; and finally, he offends Aramis by ungallantly and unintentionally bringing attention to a lady's

ROYAL GENEALOGY

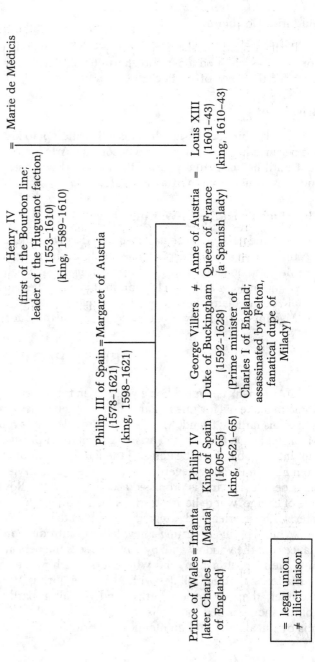

Henry IV
(first of the Bourbon line;
leader of the Huguenot faction)
(1553–1610)
(king, 1589–1610)

= Marie de Médicis

Philip III of Spain = Margaret of Austria
(1578–1621)
(king, 1598–1621)

George Villers ≠ Anne of Austria = Louis XIII
Duke of Buckingham   Queen of France   (1601–43)
(1592–1628)   (a Spanish lady)   (king, 1610–43)
(Prime minister of
Charles I of England;
assassinated by Felton,
fanatical dupe of
Milady)

Prince of Wales = Infanta   Philip IV
(later Charles I   (Maria)   King of Spain
of England)   (1605–65)
                              (king, 1621–65)

= legal union
≠ illicit liaison

MILADY'S GENEALOGY

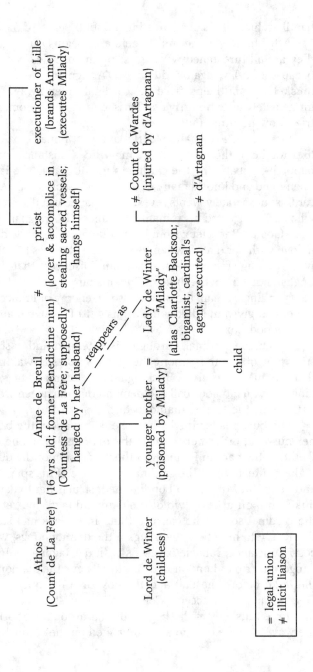

legal union
≠ illicit liaison

handkerchief. He is challenged to a duel by each of the musketeers.

After he meets the musketeers and begins dueling with Athos, they are all threatened with arrest by the dreaded cardinal's guards because of a law against dueling. D'Artagnan joins forces with the musketeers and helps drive the cardinal's men away. Thus, almost immediately after his arrival in Paris, d'Artagnan becomes an intimate friend of the three musketeers.

One day, d'Artagnan's elderly landlord, Bonacieux, comes to ask him for help; the landlord's young wife, Constance, has been kidnapped – probably by the cardinal's men because she is the queen's linen maid and knows many of the queen's secrets, secrets which the cardinal desperately wants revealed so that he can discredit the queen, who earlier rejected his romantic advances. D'Artagnan is able to rescue Madame Bonacieux from her abductors and, while doing so, falls in love with her. Later, when he inadvertently sees her cross a bridge with a strange man, he stops them and discovers that the man is an English nobleman, the duke of Buckingham, the queen's secret lover; being an Englishman, the man is also an enemy of France. That night, the queen gives the duke an elegant gift of twelve diamond tags in a rosewood box.

When the cardinal, through his extended and vast network of spies (one of whom is among the queen's ladies-in-waiting) discovers that the queen has given Buckingham the diamond tags, he asks the king to give a fabulous ball and demand that the queen wear the king's gift to her: the twelve diamond tags.

The queen is terrified when she learns about the ball and hears her husband order her to wear the diamond tags. She knows very well that they are in London, in the possession of the duke of Buckingham. Meanwhile, the cardinal sends one of his spies – the elegant and beautiful Milady – to London; he instructs her to dance with the duke, snip off at least two of the diamond tags, and return them to the cardinal so that he can use them in a blackmail scheme.

Ready to help the queen regain the diamond tags, whatever the cost, Constance Bonacieux pleads with d'Artagnan to undertake the dangerous trip to London in order to retrieve the diamond tags from the duke before the ball and thereby save the queen's reputation. D'Artagnan readily accepts Constance's request, and accompanied by the three musketeers, he begins the hazardous trip to London. On the way, they are continually ambushed by the cardinal's spies, and one by one, the musketeers are foiled from accompanying d'Artagnan to London.

When d'Artagnan reaches London, he reports the situation to Buckingham, who discovers in horror that two of the tags are missing. Immediately, he calls in his personal jeweler and instructs him to work furiously in order to make exact copies. He gives the copies to d'Artagnan, along with the remaining ten tags, and a superb, prearranged series of horses that will take d'Artagnan from London to Paris in twelve hours. Thus, the queen is able to appear in what seems to be all twelve of the diamond tags – to the utter astonishment of the cardinal. For d'Artagnan's heroic efforts, the queen secretly presents him with a large, magnificent diamond ring.

After agreeing to a rendezvous with Constance (which never takes place because she is again abducted by the cardinal's men), d'Artagnan is told that it is dangerous to remain in Paris: the cardinal knows everything that happens in Paris; it will not be long before he learns about d'Artagnan's role in the diamond tag escapade. D'Artagnan therefore decides that this would be a good time to discover what happened to his musketeer friends.

He returns to each of the places where he left them, and finding them all safe, they return to Paris – only to discover that they must buy equipment for the king's next military maneuver: the siege of La Rochelle. Each of the musketeers must find some way of getting money – something they are always short of.

While pondering how to get some cash, d'Artagnan sees Milady by accident and is overwhelmed by her beauty; he follows her and tries to protect her from a bothersome man who turns out to be her brother-in-law. The brother-in-law challenges d'Artagnan to a duel and they fight. D'Artagnan overpowers him, but spares his life. In appreciation for his life, the brother-in-law – Lord de Winter – introduces d'Artagnan to Milady, Lady de Winter. Meanwhile, Milady's maid sees d'Artagnan and falls in love with him, and later she tells him that Milady is madly in love with Count de Wardes, the man whom d'Artagnan wounded just before sailing to London. She also gives d'Artagnan a love note which Milady has written to de Wardes. D'Artagnan is so furious that he forges de Wardes' signature on a return letter to Milady, arranging a dark, nighttime rendezvous with Milady. While she thinks that she's making love to de Wardes, d'Artagnan will be making passionate love to her.

The plan works, and afterward Milady is so satisfied that she gives d'Artagnan an elegant sapphire ring surrounded with diamonds, promising to have "that stupid d'Artagnan" killed for having wounded de Wardes, the man she thinks she's been making love to in the darkness.

Later, d'Artagnan is furious, and, in order to get revenge against her, he answers another love note of hers to de Wardes, signing de Wardes' name under a flippant reminder that Milady has to "wait her turn." Milady is so incensed that she asks d'Artagnan to kill de Wardes, and as prepayment she goes to bed with him. D'Artagnan is so enamored by Milady's loveliness that he impulsively reveals that this is not the first time that he has made love to her: earlier, when she thought that she was making love in the dark to de Wardes – she wasn't. D'Artagnan was in bed with her.

Milady rears up and tries to kill d'Artagnan, and as they scuffle, her nightgown is torn and d'Artagnan sees the mark of a convict branded on one of her shoulders. The discovery of this secret is so terrible that Milady vows that d'Artagnan will die. By a stroke of good fortune, however, and some help from Kitty, d'Artagnan escapes.

Relating the adventure to Athos later, the two men discover that Milady is Athos' wife, a woman whom he thought he hanged after *he* discovered that she was a branded criminal. Athos and d'Artagnan decide to sell Milady's "tainted" ring – which originally belonged to Athos' family – and now they are both able to buy their equipment for the siege of La Rochelle. Meantime, Porthos has obtained his equipment from his aging, miserly mistress, and Aramis has obtained his equipment from his beloved friend, Madame de Chevreuse.

Before d'Artagnan and the musketeers leave in their separate regiments for the siege, the king becomes ill, and d'Artagnan's group moves out first, leaving the musketeers behind for the time being to await the king. D'Artagnan is lonesome for his friends and, one day, he wanders off alone – not a wise decision, because he is fired at by two of Milady's hired assassions. Later, during a dangerous mission that d'Artagnan is leading, the same two assassins again try to kill him. When this attempt fails, Milady decides to have some poisoned wine delivered to d'Artagnan – compliments of "the three musketeers." D'Artagnan does not realize that the wine is poisoned, and he is so busy talking that he fails to drink the wine immediately. Instead, another soldier drinks the wine – and falls dead.

Meanwhile, the three musketeers are enjoying their leisure time, drinking and joking, and, by chance, they meet the cardinal, who is going to a meeting with Milady, who is staying at the inn which the musketeers just left. The musketeers accompany the cardinal and listen through a broken stovepipe to the conversation.

Milady, they learn, is going to London to make sure that the duke of Buckingham is killed; in return, the cardinal will take revenge against d'Artagnan. The musketeers immediately decide on a plan to warn d'Artagnan and Buckingham. Thus, when Milady arrives in England, she is taken prisoner by her brother-in-law, de Winter. However, she cleverly corrupts her jailer, convinces him (a religious puritan fanatic) that Buckingham deserves to be put to death, and he obeys her.

She then escapes to France, where she is determined to complete her revenge against d'Artagnan. She goes to the convent where the queen has placed Constance Bonacieux, d'Artagnan's beloved, for protection, and there Milady wins the young girl's confidence. Precisely when d'Artagnan and the musketeers arrive to rescue Constance, Milady poisons her and escapes.

D'Artagnan and the musketeers track her down, accuse her of her many crimes — and execute her. When the entire story is revealed later to the cardinal, he is horrified at the extent of Milady's evil web of death, and he is extremely impressed with d'Artagnan's laudable actions. Consequently, he writes out a commission for d'Artagnan to become a lieutenant in the King's Musketeers. After offering the commission to Athos, Porthos, and Aramis and being refused by all three, d'Artagnan accepts the prestigious commission at the early age of twenty-one.

SUMMARIES AND COMMENTARIES

Part 1

PREFACE

This novel is one of the world's most famous adventure novels and is often referred to as the quintessential "swashbuckling" novel. Most readers throughout the Western world know something about the exploits of "the three musketeers."

In his preface, Dumas uses a literary device that was common during the romantic period in literature. That is, in order to give his novel a sense of being authentic, rather than a work of fiction, Dumas pretends that he discovered two old manuscripts, each of them written by a main character in this story. These old manuscripts, which were found in the Royal Library, supposedly tell the history of the three musketeers. The first manuscript, *Memoirs of Monsieur d'Artagnan*, was supposedly written by the most famous musketeer of all time, and the other manuscript, *Memoirs of Count de La Fère* (the novel we are about to read), was supposedly written by the musketeer Athos who was, in reality, the Count de La Fère. Thus, Dumas' *Three Musketeers*, using the device of being an old, authentic manuscript, gains credibility and immediacy by purporting to be a factual account of the daring, adventurous deeds of d'Artagnan and three of the most famous of the King's Musketeers.

CHAPTER 1

Summary

In the year 1625, in Gascony, a province of France, a young man named d'Artagnan is taking leave of his father to journey to Paris, where he will seek out the prestigious Monsieur de Tréville, captain of the King's Musketeers and a childhood friend of d'Artagnan's father.

D'Artagnan's father has only three gifts which he can give to his son: fifteen ecus in money, a ridiculous-looking horse about thirteen years old, and a letter of introduction to Monsieur de Tréville. If d'Artagnan can convince Tréville to allow him to become a musketeer, he believes that he will have his fortune made because the musketeers are a select group of swordsmen highly favored by the king.

After a sentimental leave-taking from his mother, d'Artagnan begins his journey to Paris. He arrives at the market town of Meung, where he sees an unknown nobleman who he believes is laughing at him, or at least at his horse. D'Artagnan's impetuous temper causes him to insult the nobleman and pick a quarrel with him. D'Artagnan is outnumbered, however, and before long he is carried unconscious into the inn. Learning from the innkeeper that d'Artagnan has a letter to the powerful Monsieur de Tréville, the nobleman steals it from d'Artagnan's doublet.

When d'Artagnan recovers, he goes downstairs in time to see the nobleman talking with someone whom he addresses as "Milady." Later, d'Artagnan discovers that his letter of recommendation to Tréville is missing, and after threatening the innkeeper and his servants, he learns that the mysterious nobleman ransacked his belongings and apparently stole the valuable letter of introduction. D'Artagnan departs, and when he arrives in Paris, he rents a room that he discovers is near the home of Monsieur de Tréville.

Commentary

This first chapter moves quickly. We see that our hero is a country boy, unaccustomed to the sophisticated ways outside of his little town; he is also from a section of France which is famous for its brave and daring young men. Throughout the novel, d'Artagnan's birthplace will be referred to as a place famous for producing men of exceptional courage, military valor, and quick tempers. D'Artagnan possesses all of these qualities – especially the latter. In fact, in the opening chapters of this novel, we see that d'Artagnan is so impetuous that he quickly embroils himself in a series of duels with three of the king's best swordsmen.

D'Artagnan's encounter with the as-yet-unnamed Count de Rochefort introduces us to the man who will become d'Artagnan's mysterious nemesis (enemy). However, until the end of the novel, Rochefort will be referred to only as "the man from Meung." At the end of the novel, when ordered to do so by Cardinal Richelieu, Rochefort and d'Artagnan will put aside their differences and become allies and friends.

The puzzling appearance here of "Milady" will become even more important to the plot than d'Artagnan's chance encounter with Rochefort; Milady will play a major, pivotal role later in the novel. The ultimate importance of both of these mysterious characters suggests that Dumas had the plot of his novel well outlined before he began writing it.

CHAPTERS 2–4

Summary

Monsieur de Tréville, the captain of the King's Musketeers, is a genuine and loyal friend to the king, who in turn thoroughly values Tréville's loyalty and devotion. Tréville began his career as a brave, loyal young Gascon, one very much like d'Artagnan, and now, as captain of the King's Musketeers, he holds one of the country's most powerful and prestigious posts. In fact, the King's Musketeers have become so famous that Cardinal Richelieu, not to be outdone by the king, has established his own company of guards; both men, the king and the cardinal, searched throughout the French countryside for the bravest and most courageous men.

When d'Artagnan calls upon Monsieur de Tréville, he finds a number of musketeers awaiting audiences with this powerful man, and he listens in particular to two musketeers who are bantering with each other in a friendly manner. One of them is Porthos, dressed rather pompously; the other is Aramis, dressed more conservatively. Aramis states that he is waiting for the queen to have an heir to the throne; afterward, he will resign from the musketeers and begin studying for the priesthood. Their conversation is interrupted when it is announced that Monsieur de Tréville will receive d'Artagnan.

As d'Artagnan enters, he sees that Monsieur de Tréville is in a bad mood. The exalted gentleman immediately calls for Athos, Porthos, and Aramis. Porthos and Aramis enter and are told that the cardinal informed the king that they, as well as Athos, were arrested by the cardinal's guards in a tavern where they were causing a disturbance. Coolly, but inwardly enraged, Tréville vows that he "won't have [his] musketeers going to low taverns, picking quarrels, fighting in the street, and being laughed at by the cardinal's guards."

Porthos explains that they were taken by surprise, that two of their group were killed, and that Athos was wounded before they had a chance to draw their swords – thus, it was six against three. Yet even with those odds, Aramis killed one of the cardinal's guards with the guard's own sword. At that moment, the wounded and pale Athos appears, but before he can say much, he collapses. Tréville sends for doctors to have Athos tended to and dismisses the two musketeers.

Alone with Tréville, d'Artagnan describes his desire to be a musketeer, the letter of introduction that was stolen, and the mysterious nobleman who stole it. Tréville is curious; he asks d'Artagnan to describe the man, and afterward Tréville is sure of the man's identity: the unidentified nobleman is none other than the cardinal's right-hand man (later identified as Count de Rochefort). D'Artagnan asks for the name of the mysterious nobleman, but Tréville refuses to reveal it.

He tells d'Artagnan to forget the man and to walk on the other side of the street – if necessary – to avoid him.

D'Artagnan then describes the woman whom the nobleman referred to as "Milady," and it is obvious that Tréville also knows the identity of the mysterious lady. Tréville turns to write a letter commending d'Artagnan to the Royal Academy when d'Artagnan suddenly spies the mysterious "man from Meung" across the street. Without waiting for the letter of recommendation, he rushes out.

Running after the mystery man, d'Artagnan inadvertently collides with Athos, reinjuring Athos' wounded shoulder; Athos is furious and challenges d'Artagnan to a duel at noon. Still chasing the mysterious "man from Meung," d'Artagnan runs headlong into the pompous Porthos and discovers that his magnificent golden shoulder belt is a fraud; it is only partly gold. Infuriated, Porthos challenges d'Artagnan to a duel at 1 P.M. Again, d'Artagnan takes up the pursuit, only to discover that he has lost his man. At this very moment, though, he sees Aramis talking to some other musketeers, and he notices that Aramis is standing on a lady's elegant handkerchief. D'Artagnan retrieves the handkerchief and gives it to Aramis, who glares at him. After the guards leave, Aramis reprimands d'Artagnan for being so "ungallant" and bringing attention to the lady's handkerchief. He promises to teach d'Artagnan a lesson; he challenges him to a duel at 2 P.M.

Commentary

Dumas stresses the importance of d'Artagnan's being a Gascon by paralleling his early years with Tréville's early years. Like d'Artagnan, Tréville is also a Gascon. Possessing the same courageous and adventuresome qualities that d'Artagnan possesses, Tréville has risen to be one of the most powerful men in France. Thus we can anticipate that d'Artagnan, who is also endowed with quick-witted daring, shrewd, intelligent bravery, and courageous loyalty, will use these qualities to become a success in Paris.

In this world of the 1620s, perhaps the most significant attribute that both Tréville and d'Artagnan possess is their absolute sense of loyalty and devotion to either a person or a cause. Indeed, Tréville's absolute devotion to his king is part of his power. Likewise, we will soon see that d'Artagnan is the type of man who is absolutely loyal to his friends; in the upcoming episode when the king gives d'Artagnan forty pistoles, d'Artagnan immediately divides the money with Athos,

Porthos, and Aramis because of his instantaneous sense of loyalty to them. Later, d'Artagnan's devotion and loyalty to the queen will motivate many of his actions.

Since Athos, Porthos, and Aramis – the three musketeers – share many similarities, it is important to note their differences. All of them have assumed aliases, but we sense that only Athos has noble blood; he conducts himself as a young nobleman might. Porthos, on the other hand, relishes in the intrigues of society, and he prides himself on his many romantic conquests; later, when he is in need of money, he will use his charm and good looks to obtain money from a wealthy woman. In contrast, Aramis is passing his time as a musketeer only until the queen provides an heir for the realm; afterward, Aramis will enter the priesthood. There are many other differences in the men that will be noted later, but, for the present, these differences are sufficient to help us readily distinguish one from the other.

Ironically, just as d'Artagnan is about to receive Tréville's recommendation for the Royal Academy, the mysterious "man from Meung" reenters d'Artagnan's life – causing d'Artagnan to dash out of Tréville's house without the new letter of recommendation. In only minutes, d'Artagnan re-wounds Athos, rushes into the proud Porthos and reveals the man's fraudulent golden shoulder belt, and, finally, he contradicts Aramis about the ownership of a lady's batiste handkerchief. In less than twenty-four hours after arriving in Paris, d'Artagnan finds himself challenged to duels by three of the greatest swordsmen in France.

CHAPTER 5

Summary

On his way back to meet Athos, d'Artagnan ponders his situation. If he wounds the already-wounded Athos, he will look bad; yet if he himself is wounded by the already-wounded Athos, he will be doubly disgraced. He searches for a way out of the dilemma. Arriving on time for the duel, he finds that Athos' seconds have not arrived. Meanwhile, Athos' shoulder has begun to throb painfully, so d'Artagnan offers him some of his mother's miraculous salve. This generosity impresses Athos. Afterward, the seconds arrive: Porthos and Aramis. D'Artagnan registers great surprise when he learns that these gentlemen are known as "the three inseparables," or "the three musketeers."

Just as Athos and d'Artagnan have their swords in position for the duel, they are interrupted by five of the cardinal's guards and are ordered to yield to arrest because of the edict against dueling. D'Artagnan has to decide whether he will support the cardinal's men (after all, the cardinal is more powerful than the king) or whether he should side with the King's Musketeers. Immediately, he decides on the musketeers. During the encounter, the cardinal's guards are soundly defeated, and d'Artagnan is accepted into the close camaraderie of Athos, Porthos, and Aramis.

Commentary

Prior to each of d'Artagnan's dueling encounters with the three musketeers, Dumas creates tension by making us guess how the hero will confront each of them and yet emerge with honor from each encounter. This question, of course, is ultimately obviated by the appearance of the cardinal's guards and by d'Artagnan's decision to fight on the side of the musketeers. His brilliant although unorthodox swordsmanship wins him the respect of the musketeers, and thus through a stroke of luck, d'Artagnan becomes, as it were, an unofficial "fourth musketeer." Not until later in the novel, however, will he become an official musketeer.

CHAPTERS 6–7

Summary

Hearing how the three musketeers and d'Artagnan fought with five of the cardinal's guards and left four of them lying on the ground, King Louis calls in Monsieur de Tréville for an explanation. The king pretends to be angry, but he is secretly pleased that his musketeers defeated the cardinal's guards. In particular, he wants to have an audience with d'Artagnan, the young Gascon who fought so daringly.

The next day, the three musketeers and d'Artagnan spend the morning playing tennis. D'Artagnan doesn't know how to play the game, and after retiring to the sidelines, he is insulted by one of the cardinal's most gifted swordsmen, Bernajoux. During a duel, d'Artagnan overpowers the superior swordsman, but he is attacked by others, and soon, musketeers and cardinalists are embroiled in a free-for-all brawl. The three musketeers, however, are able to extract themselves because they have a noontime meeting with the king; unfortunately, His Majesty went hunting that morning after one of the cardinal's men told him that there was a magnificent stag in a neighboring woods.

By the time that Tréville is able to have an audience with the king, Louis has heard about this new brawl with the cardinal's guards. Tréville is able to prove, though, that the cardinal's men provoked the quarrel and were soundly defeated. The king then has an audience with the three musketeers and d'Artagnan and hears d'Artagnan describe in detail the events of the preceding days. Satisfied, the king rewards d'Artagnan with forty pistoles, which d'Artagnan divides with the three musketeers.

In Chapter 7, d'Artagnan asks for advice concerning how he should spend his share of the forty pistoles; Athos tells him to have a good meal, Porthos tells him to hire a servant, and Aramis tells him to take a mistress. D'Artagnan hires a servant named Planchet, who serves them all a fine meal. We then learn more about the musketeers.

Athos, although handsome and intelligent, lives a quiet life with Grimaud; they virtually never speak to one another. Porthos, however, is different; he is loud and outgoing, and his servant Mousqueton is also loud and rough. Aramis is the most reserved of the three, and his servant, Bazin, is a pious fellow who looks forward to Aramis' entering the priesthood.

When d'Artagnan enters the king's company of guards, under Monsieur des Essarts, the three musketeers often accompany d'Artagnan on his guard duties. Very soon, the four are constantly seen together.

Commentary

As stated earlier in the novel, the only way for a poor young man from Gascony to make his fortune is to have the courage, daring, and bravery to attract the attention of powerful people. Fortunately, fate arranges matters so that d'Artagnan is confronted by members of the cardinal's guard, who have the reputation of being expert swordsmen. The fact that so young a man defeats so experienced and polished a swordsman as the cardinalist Bernajoux attracts the attention of the king himself, who rewards d'Artagnan and requests that the young Gascon be placed in special troops, an honor which will lead to d'Artagnan's later becoming a musketeer.

The modern reader is often perplexed at the blatant disregard for human life that is so often found in this "swashbuckling" type of novel, but it is a common characteristic of the genre; d'Artagnan himself seems to have little or no regard for his own life as long as he dies an honorable death at the hands of someone whom he considers noble.

Part 2

CHAPTERS 8–9

Summary

The forty pistoles received from the king are soon spent, and although the musketeers receive an advance on their pay from Tréville, they are soon broke. Thus they start enumerating people whom they have entertained in the past in order to be invited to meals. When they are beginning to become desperate, d'Artagnan receives an unusual visitor. His landlord, Monsieur Bonacieux, seeks help; his wife, Constance, the queen's linen maid, has been mysteriously abducted – probably for political reasons. Constance is the goddaughter of Monsieur de La Porte, the queen's gentleman-in-waiting; it was through this powerful and influential gentleman that Madame Bonacieux received her position. Both Constance and La Porte are known to be extremely devoted and loyal to the queen (whose heritage is Spanish, whose husband is French, and whose title is Anne of Austria).

During d'Artagnan's discussion with Monsieur Bonacieux, we learn that Bonacieux is d'Artagnan's landlord and that d'Artagnan is several months behind with his rent. But Bonacieux has another reason for coming to see d'Artagnan; Bonacieux is a coward, and he has often seen d'Artagnan duel in the company of the three musketeers, who are known to be brave and expert with their swords.

As they are discussing Bonacieux's predicament, d'Artagnan suddenly sees "the man from Meung" across the street and dashes out to confront him, but returns half an hour later, having had no success.

D'Artagnan explains to Athos and Porthos that "a woman has been abducted . . . and probably threatened and may be tortured, and all because she is faithful to her mistress, the queen." We then learn that the queen is being persecuted by the cardinal for being loyal to her native Spain (an enemy of France); in addition, she is in love with the duke of Buckingham, an Englishman (England is also an enemy of France). Nonetheless, the musketeers agree: the queen, despite her emotional and political bonds, must be defended.

Guards appear and arrest Bonacieux, and rather than defend him and cast suspicion on himself, d'Artagnan allows Bonacieux to be arrested. The musketeers and d'Artagnan agree to try to free Madame Bonacieux because she is loyal to the queen and is the goddaughter of Monsieur de La Porte.

Commentary

The title of Chapter 8, "A Court Intrigue," characterizes the action of much of this novel. For many of Dumas' early readers, a court intrigue was as exciting as a salacious story in today's *National Enquirer*, or some other gossip tabloid. Court intrigues and gossip have always fascinated many readers – in Dumas' day as well as in the present.

At the beginning of this chapter, Dumas again emphasizes the motto of the three musketeers; each shares whatever money he has with the others and thus fulfills their motto: "All for one, one for all." By now, d'Artagnan knows that if any difficulty or need arises, he can count on the three musketeers.

The introduction of Constance Bonacieux begins one of the many sub-plots of the novel. She will move in and out of the action until her untimely death late in the novel. She will be d'Artagnan's first love, creating resolute loyalty and adoration in the young Gascon.

Chapter 8 ends with the sudden reappearance of the mysterious "man [in a cloak] from Meung," an appearance which neatly fits the "cloak and dagger" type of novel, another category into which this novel readily belongs.

For d'Artagnan and the three musketeers, the mere fact that a lady who is close to the queen has been abducted is reason enough for them to pledge their talents to solving the mystery of her disappearance. And to facilitate matters, they allow her older husband to be arrested on false charges so that he won't interfere with their actions (and won't be bothering d'Artagnan with such "insignificant" matters as the rent). The chapter concludes with their agreeing on the motto, "All for one, one for all."

Summary

The term "mousetrap" is explained as being a method whereby the police trap friends and/or associates of a person who has been arrested for political reasons. Here, the authorities have placed four guards at Monsieur Bonacieux's house, and they plan to arrest anyone who knocks. Meanwhile, upstairs, d'Artagnan has removed most of the first section of the flooring in his apartment so that he can hear the entire proceedings. When he hears the guards manhandling Constance Bonacieux, he sends his servant, Planchet, to enlist the aid of the three musketeers, and grabbing his sword, he flies to Constance's rescue. Only one of the guards is armed, and after a short time, d'Artagnan is able to drive all four men from the premises in a manner so dashing and thrilling that Constance is marvelously impressed and eternally grateful.

Constance Bonacieux turns out to be young (in her early twenties), charming, and beautiful. When she describes the man who abducted her, d'Artagnan recognizes him as "the man from Meung." She tells d'Artagnan about her escape: she was left alone, so she immediately tied some sheets together and let herself down from a window. She feels so deeply grateful to d'Artagnan that she entrusts him with a secret password which will gain him entrance into the palace to see Monsieur de La Porte, whom he is to send to her. When d'Artagnan delivers the message to La Porte, the gentleman advises him to find someone whose clock is slow and go there and establish an alibi.

Afterward, d'Artagnan daydreams about a romantic love affair with Constance Bonacieux, and while wandering idly through the Paris streets, he finds himself outside Aramis' house, where he sees a lady in a cloak knocking at what appears to be Aramis' window. He sees the woman talking to another woman, and when she leaves, he discovers that it is Constance Bonacieux. He follows her and accosts her. She denies knowing Aramis, and when she refuses to reveal the secret of her mission, d'Artagnan offers to escort her to her destination. She permits him to do so on condition that he leave and not follow her. D'Artagnan promises and returns home, where he learns that Athos has been arrested by authorities who thought that they were arresting d'Artagnan.

D'Artagnan sets out for Tréville's house to tell him about the arrest and other events. On a bridge, he sees two figures—one is dressed exactly like Constance Bonacieux and the other is in a musketeer's uniform; his appearance resembles Aramis. When d'Artagnan brashly stops them, calling out Aramis' name, he discovers that Constance Bonacieux is escorting the duke of Buckingham to the Louvre Palace. D'Artagnan is pleased to escort them safely to the palace.

At the palace, Constance leads the duke through a series of corridors and leaves him in a private anteroom. Soon, Anne of Austria, the queen of France, appears, and the duke makes his protestations of love to her, but she continually and sadly rejects his overtures, even though she is obviously in love with him. As a parting gift for him, she goes to her chambers and returns with a rosewood box as a token of her love. Inside the rosewood box are twelve diamond tags, or studs (button-like ornaments).

Commentary

Here, as part of the novel of intrigue, we are introduced to the villainous "authorities" who set a trap and arrest anyone—innocent or guilty—who enters the "mousetrap." In modern terms, this is similar to police entrapment, a technique whereby the police use an officer to trap someone into violating a law so that the police can arrest that person. It is by this method that d'Artagnan meets Constance Bonacieux, who becomes his first love.

Constance Bonacieux's escape from her captors (by tying sheets together and letting herself down from a window) and d'Artagnan's rescue of her are in the best swashbuckling, romantic tradition, as is the scene where the four guards battle against d'Artagnan and d'Artagnan overcomes these odds and rescues the fair damsel in distress.

Also in the tradition of the troubadors and other devoted cavaliers who love for-the-sake-of-love, d'Artagnan immediately falls in love with Constance Bonacieux; she will be d'Artagnan's beloved for whom he will perform valorous deeds. His relationship with Constance Bonacieux will, of course, eventually cause him to volunteer to perform a great service for the queen, thereby saving her honor and virtue. Ultimately, then, d'Artagnan's love and devotion to Constance Bonacieux will be one of the causes for his own advancement in society and will tightly entangle him in the deadly political intrigues of France. In other words, the relationship established here and intensified when d'Artagnan helps Constance Bonacieux slip the duke of Buckingham into the Louvre are sufficient for Constance to trust d'Artagnan to go on the dangerous and highly secret mission for the queen.

The importance of this love affair is a commentary on the times. Dumas writes that Constance Bonacieux was an amorous ideal, that she knew the secrets of the court and was not insensitive to masculine attentions, even though she was married. Furthermore, it was the custom of the time for a young and handsome man to take money or other gifts from his mistress, and the young and handsome d'Artagnan is always in need of money.

The scene where d'Artagnan sees the mysterious woman in a cloak, knocking at what he thinks is Aramis' window is an example of a scene which allows the reader to classify this novel as a "cloak and dagger" novel – that is, mysterious people are often seen half-concealed by cloaks, and they do not reveal themselves until someone has drawn his sword, as does d'Artagnan in this scene.

Chapter 12 presents our first view of George Villiers, the English duke of Buckingham – an extremely handsome and sophisticated man. The love which Buckingham has for the French queen is depicted in terms of his desperate need to be with her. There is no compromise of the queen's honor – except, at the end of the interview, she gives him a gift as a token of her love for him. This gift, a monogrammed, gold-inlaid jewel box made of rosewood, is, as we later discover, filled with diamond tags, or studs, which will become the object of the first real adventure in the novel, when the king demands that the queen wear the jewels to a ball. The king, however, demands that the queen wear the diamonds only because the cardinal tells him that the jewels are in Buckingham's possession; the cardinal wants to prove that the queen is untrue so that he can gain even more power over the king.

CHAPTERS 13–16

Summary

We return to the fate of Monsieur Bonacieux, who has been taken to prison and questioned by the authorities about his wife. As it turns out, Bonacieux is much more concerned about his own avarice and safety than he is about his wife. He explains that his only interest in d'Artagnan was that he needed someone who could help him find his wife. When Athos is brought in, Bonacieux tells them that this man is *not* d'Artagnan. Bonacieux is then taken from the prison, placed in a carriage, and taken for a trip which he assumes is a ride to the gallows.

Later, Bonacieux is questioned by someone whom he discovers to be the powerful and imminent Cardinal Richelieu. While interrogating Bonacieux, the cardinal discovers that the houses which Bonacieux visited with his wife – houses which Constance Bonacieux had said were merchants' houses – are, in reality, the two houses where the duke of Buckingham and the queen's trusted friend, Madame de Chevreuse, have been hiding. When the cardinal calls in Count de Rochefort, Bonacieux immediately cries out that Rochefort is the man who abducted Constance.

Rochefort reports that the cardinal's spy in the queen's inner circle, Madame de Lannoy, has reported that the queen left her ladies-in-waiting and was gone for awhile. When she returned, she was carrying a rosewood box containing the diamond tags which the king gave her. She went into the antechamber and when she returned, she was empty-handed. The cardinal is certain that the duke of Buckingham has the coveted box and the diamond tags.

When Bonacieux is recalled and questioned further by the cardinal, the old man becomes putty in the hands of the honey-tongued cardinal; Bonacieux pledges everlasting loyalty to him. The cardinal then sends one of his men with a letter to be delivered to a woman in England, a certain Milady, who is to dance with Buckingham and secretly snip off two of the diamond tags that he will be wearing.

The next day, d'Artagnan tells Tréville about Athos' mistaken arrest. Tréville goes to see the king about Athos' arrest and discovers that the cardinal is already there; after much discussion, during which Tréville vouches for the whereabouts of both Athos and d'Artagnan during the fracas with Bonacieux, the king and the cardinal both agree to let the matter rest.

Immediately after Tréville leaves, the cardinal informs the king that Buckingham is in Paris. The king is certain that with the help of Madame de Chevreuse, the queen and the duke are seeing one another. When he hears that the queen has been writing letters that very morning, he is determined to have her searched and have the letters brought to him. He goes to see the queen and informs her that his chancellor, Seguier, will visit her soon and, at his command, will make a request of her. When Chancellor Seguier appears and searches the queen's room and desk and finds nothing, he prepares to search her person. The queen indignantly refuses, and he is about to use force when she reaches into her bosom and gives him a letter.

When the king opens the letter, he discovers that it is not a love letter to Buckingham; it is a political letter. The queen is asking her brother in Spain and her brother, the Emperor of Austria, to demand the dismissal of Cardinal Richelieu. The cardinal, upon reading the letter, cleverly offers to resign, but the king knows that he cannot manage France without the cardinal's powerful influence.

To make peace with the queen, the cardinal suggests that since the queen loves to dance, the king should give a big ball, and he tells the king that he should *insist* that the queen wear the diamond tags that he gave her as a present. On returning home, the cardinal hears from Milady that she has secured two diamond tags; she needs money to get to Paris, and as soon as she gets the money, she will be in Paris in four or five days. The cardinal then plots the date of the ball so that he might trap the queen.

Commentary

In Chapter 13, we find out that Constance Bonacieux is only twenty-three years old; since she is married to a fifty-one-year-old stingy, selfish husband, she would naturally make a likely candidate for a love affair with d'Artagnan, especially since we also learn that her husband thinks of his love for his wife as being secondary to his love for money and influence. Bonacieux is thus an easy prey for the powerful cardinal, and he quickly becomes the cardinal's dupe. Later, when Constance asks him to do a service for the queen, he will *not* consent to it; thus, she turns to our hero, d'Artagnan, and asks him to perform this crucial deed for the queen.

In his questioning of Monsieur Bonacieux, the cardinal is seen to have an acute sense of the intrigues of the court. He knows that the duke of Buckingham is in Paris, and he is able to discover where both the duke and Madame de Chevreuse are staying – that is, in the houses that Constance Bonacieux often visited, pretending to her husband that she was visiting "tradesmen." Through his spies, the cardinal is able to deduce that the queen gave Buckingham the rosewood box containing the diamond tags. Knowing this, he requests the king to give a ball and *demand* that the queen wear the diamond tags. This demand, as we soon will see, will require d'Artagnan to go on his first adventure. He will have to get the diamond tags and return them to the queen *before* the date of the ball, a date which the cardinal sets as soon has he hears that his spy, Milady, has stolen two of the diamond tags – snipped them off while she was dancing with Buckingham.

In an earlier chapter, when d'Artagnan helped get a message to Monsieur de La Porte, the gentleman told d'Artagnan to find someone with a slow clock who could provide him with an alibi. D'Artagnan went to see Tréville and reset his clock; now, when Tréville has to give his word of honor that d'Artagnan was with him at a precise hour, he can do so – fully believing that he is telling the truth. Consequently, d'Artagnan is freed from all accusations by the cardinal.

Until Chapter 16, the reader might have wondered why the queen is such an enemy of the cardinal. It has been suggested that there are two reasons: (1) she is Spanish and Spain is France's enemy, and (2) she loves Buckingham, an Englishman, and England is an enemy of France. However, in Chapter 16, the real reason appears: ". . . the queen [Anne of Austria] was persecuted by the cardinal because he could not forgive her for having rejected his amorous advances."

Because of the cardinal's accusations about Anne's affair with Buckingham, the king is certain that his wife is untrue. He orders that her person be searched, and in those days, a gentleman's having his wife searched for a love letter was a dastardly thing, but a *king's* having the *queen* searched was beyond comprehension. Thus, the cardinal, whose rumors cleverly prompt the search, now urges the king to be reconciled with the queen. Cunningly, he suggests a festive ball so that the queen will *have* to wear the diamond tags, which are – he feels sure – in the possession of the duke of Buckingham. Now the trap for the queen is set, and to counteract this trap, d'Artagnan will have to undertake the journey to recover the diamond tags and return them to the queen.

CHAPTERS 17–19

Summary

The king wonders briefly why the cardinal is so insistent that the queen wear the diamond tags, but he nevertheless tells the queen about his plans for the ball and instructs her to wear the diamond tags. On further questioning, the queen learns that the idea of having a ball was the cardinal's idea; furthermore, it was the cardinal who suggested that she wear the diamond tags.

After the king leaves, the queen is filled with fear. Suddenly, Constance Bonacieux enters from the closet and reveals that she knows the entire story; furthermore, she promises that she will find someone to go to the duke of Buckingham and retrieve the diamond tags. The queen reminds Constance that a letter would have to accompany the messenger and, if intercepted, she (the queen) would be ruined — divorced and exiled. Constance, not knowing of her own husband's allegiance to the cardinal, swears that her husband will do anything for her. Relieved, the queen gives Constance a jewel to sell in order to defray the expenses of the journey.

At home, Constance discovers that her husband has become an ardent cardinalist and will have nothing to do with her intrigues: "Your queen is a treacherous Spanish woman, and whatever the cardinal does is right," he says. Constance also discovers that her husband is in league with Count de Rochefort, even though he knows that Rochefort is the person who abducted Constance. Monsieur Bonacieux leaves and Constance is certain that he will betray her.

D'Artagnan overhears the entire conversation between husband and wife, and later he is delighted to assert that her husband is a wretch. He then offers himself at her service. When Constance is reluctant to tell d'Artagnan all of the details about the mission, he reminds her that she was about to tell her traitorous husband everything, and furthermore, d'Artagnan loves her more than her husband does.

Constance relents and tells him all about the secret mission, and d'Artagnan promises to obtain a leave of absence and be on his way to London. Constance suddenly remembers the three hundred pistoles that the cardinal gave her husband, and she gives the money to d'Artagnan for the journey. D'Artagnan is delighted: "It will be twice as amusing to save the queen with His Eminence's [the cardinal's] money."

At that moment, they hear her husband returning with someone. D'Artagnan recognizes the person as "the man from Meung," and he is ready to attack him when Constance stops him because of his duty to the queen; in other words, first things first. They listen and overhear her husband's plan to supposedly relent and agree to go on the errand for his wife; then, after he has the queen's letter to Buckingham, he will take it to the cardinal.

On his way to Tréville's house, d'Artagnan wonders if he should tell Tréville about the secret mission; interestingly, Tréville tells d'Artagnan to keep the details of the mission secret and, instead, to ask for whatever favors he needs. D'Artagnan says that the cardinal will do anything to keep him from getting to London, and Tréville suggests that at least four people should go on the journey so that one of them might succeed in actually getting there. D'Artagnan says that Athos, Porthos, and Aramis will accompany him without demanding to know the nature of the secret mission. Accordingly, Tréville writes out passes, and d'Artagnan goes to each of the musketeers and tells them to get ready for the trip. They discuss several tactics for successfully accomplishing the mission, but d'Artagnan tells them that they must all go together, not in separate directions, because if one of them is killed, the others can make certain that the letter is finally delivered to London. They agree and begin to make preparations to leave.

Commentary

When the queen is instructed to wear her diamond tags to the ball, she is also told that it was the cardinal who proposed having the ball. Constance quickly realizes that the idea of her wearing the diamond tags was also the cardinal's idea. As a consequence, she knows that the cardinal has a spy among one of her ladies-in-waiting, but she does not know which one. Therefore, when Constance Bonacieux appears from the closet, where she has been tending to the linen, she could have overheard the conversation between the queen and the king; therefore, the queen is not sure, at first, if she can trust Constance. But after Constance's protestations of loyalty and her reminder that she is the person who brought Buckingham to her, the queen is finally convinced that she can trust Constance. Now we can see that these earlier episodes function as a basis for Constance's loyalty and are proof that the cardinal is indeed a powerful enemy of the queen.

In a similar way, we can now look back at other scenes. For example, when we read that Constance Bonacieux discovered that her husband was a cardinalist—totally devoted to and committed to the cardinal—we realize now how the cardinal used his interview with

Constance's stupid husband in order to gain another loyal adherent.

Dumas closes Chapter 18 with a brilliant stroke of irony: the old miser Bonacieux is howling for his missing money. D'Artagnan's trip to London will be financed by money which the cardinal gave to Bonacieux.

Clearly, Dumas delights in d'Artagnan's heroics. In the scene where Constance is in despair, fearing that the mission for the queen is doomed to fail, Dumas uses the romantic device of having d'Artagnan overhear the entire conversation between Constance and her husband; then, suddenly and romantically, d'Artagnan presents himself as her rescuer and savior. The queen's honor can be preserved.

Note too how Dumas uses a combination of circumstances in order for d'Artagnan to be fully characterized as the romantic hero: he is in the right place at the right time and overhears the right kind of intrigue so that he can become involved in the affairs of great people. Dumas also stresses that it is *d'Artagnan's* plan for the mission that the older, more experienced musketeers finally accept. D'Artagnan is younger than the other men, but already he seems to have a natural talent for intrigue and adventure; in fact, Buckingham will later marvel at d'Artagnan's being so young, yet so dashing, brave, and inventive.

CHAPTERS 20–22

Summary

At 2 A.M., the four adventurers, accompanied by their armed servants, ride out of Paris. At the first inn where they stop, Porthos gets into an argument with a stranger; his companions are anxious to be on their way, so they tell him to "kill that man and rejoin us as soon as you can." They continue on their journey and decide to wait two hours for Porthos, but he never appears.

Later, they encounter eight or nine men working on the road, and suddenly the workmen race for the ditch, pick up their muskets, and begin firing. D'Artagnan realizes that they have ridden into an ambush, so he warns the others, urging them back. Mousqueton falls, wounded. Aramis receives wounds and can't ride any farther, so they leave him at an inn in Crèvecoeur, tended to by his servant, Bazin.

The original party of eight is now reduced to four: d'Artagnan and his servant Planchet, and Athos and his servant Grimaud. At midnight they reach Amiens and stop at the Lis d'Or inn. Grimaud guards the horses while Planchet sleeps in front of the door so that d'Artagnan and Athos won't be taken by surprise. Two hours later, they are awakened by noises, and at 4 A.M., they hear more loud noises in the stable. They investigate and discover Grimaud lying unconscious with a bleeding head. Planchet goes to saddle the horses but they are still too exhausted to go any farther. Mousqueton's horse has even been bled, mistakenly, by the local veterinarian.

When Athos goes to pay the bill, the innkeeper looks at the money and declares it to be counterfeit. At this moment, four armed men rush toward him, but Athos holds them off while yelling to d'Artagnan to escape.

Outside Calais, both d'Artagnan's and Planchet's horses collapse when they are only a hundred paces from the town gates. They dismount and begin following a young nobleman and his servant. By accident, they overhear a ship's captain stating that he will take no one to England without the written permission of the cardinal. The young nobleman presents a paper signed by the cardinal and is told that the paper must be endorsed by the harbor master.

D'Artagnan and Planchet continue following the two men, pick a quarrel with them, and while Planchet duels with the servant, d'Artagnan duels with the young nobleman. Defeating him, even though he is wounded while doing so, d'Artagnan steals the traveling permit, which is made out to Count de Wardes. He gets the permit signed by the harbor master, takes it to the ship's captain, and he and Planchet sail for England.

For a moment in London, d'Artagnan is at a loss: he knows no English. Nonetheless, he writes the duke of Buckingham's name on a piece of paper and is immediately directed to the duke's residence. The duke's servant, who speaks French, takes d'Artagnan to the field where the duke is hunting with the king. When the duke reads the letter that d'Artagnan gives him, he turns pale and immediately returns to London.

On the ride back to London, d'Artagnan relates his exploits, surprising the duke that someone so young could be so brave, resolute, and resourceful. The duke takes d'Artagnan through many rooms and finally to a concealed chapel, where he shows him a life-sized portrait of the queen of France. Then, as he takes the diamond tags out of their box, he is horrified to see that two of them are missing. He instantly realizes that the ribbons have been cut, and he knows that the diamonds were taken by Milady – Lady de Winter – obviously an agent for the cardinal. Immediately, he sends for his jeweler and his secretary.

He instructs his secretary to have all the English ports closed so that Milady cannot return to France with the diamond tags. When d'Artagnan reveals his astonishment at the duke's enormous, unlimited power and his use of it – all for the sake of his beloved, Anne of Austria, queen of France – Buckingham acknowledges that "Anne of Austria is my true queen. At a word from her, I'd betray my country, my king, even my God." D'Artagnan marvels at such total devotion.

The jeweler arrives and tells Buckingham that duplicating copies of the missing diamonds will take a week; Buckingham offers him double the price if he can finish the job in two days, and he agrees to do so. Since speed is of the utmost importance, the jeweler immediately goes to work in the duke's palace. D'Artagnan is again impressed by the duke's power and his ardent love for the French queen.

After the fake diamond tags are made, the duke wants to reward d'Artagnan, but d'Artagnan reminds the duke that he, d'Artagnan, is serving the queen of France and that some day in the future, he and the duke might be enemies on the battlefield. However, because Buckingham sincerely wants to reward him and because d'Artagnan needs some good horses in order to return to Paris in time for the ball, d'Artagnan accepts four magnificent horses – one for d'Artagnan himself and one for each of the three musketeers. D'Artagnan is also given the secret password that will enable him to change horses. Twelve hours later, he is in Paris.

Next day, all of Paris is talking about the upcoming ball. That night, the king is especially pleased to see that the queen is wearing her diamond tags. The cardinal, however, calls the king's attention to the fact that the queen has only *ten* tags. He gives two diamond tags to the king and tells him to inquire of the queen about the two tags which are missing. During their next dance together, the king is unable to count the number of diamond tags on his wife, so at the end of the dance, he tells her that two of her tags are missing – and he gives her two more. The queen triumphantly announces that now she has fourteen! The king counts the tags: she is wearing twelve – and now she does have two more diamond tags. The cardinal is stunned at the news, but recovers from his astonishment and explains to the king that the two extra diamond tags are his way of making a gift to the queen. Anne is not fooled, however, and she subtly lets the cardinal know that *his* two diamond tags probably cost him *more* than the king's original twelve.

Later, d'Artagnan is rewarded for his success in returning the tags; Constance Bonacieux leads him down a series of corridors where the queen presents her hand to be kissed. As d'Artagnan does so, she presses a magnificent ring into his hand. Constance then returns and tells d'Artagnan that she left a note for him at his house.

Commentary

Again, we can see why this novel is called one of the best swash-buckling, "cloak and dagger" adventure novels. In Chapter 20, the four adventurers embark on a mission and encounter all sorts of un-expected obstacles. Without a doubt, the cardinal seems to be able to know exactly what everyone in the kingdom is doing. Remember that Tréville warned d'Artagnan about this very possibility.

On the trip to London, the musketeers and d'Artagnan encounter difficulty at the first inn and leave Porthos. Then during an ambush along the road, they believe that Mousqueton is killed; they know that Aramis is wounded, so they leave him at an inn, tended by his servant, Bazin. Later, Athos is falsely accused by an innkeeper of try-ing to pass counterfeit money and is attacked by four men. Finally, when d'Artagnan and his servant reach the port of Calais, they dis-cover that the cardinal has had the port closed and is sending one of his men, Count de Wardes, with a special permit to London. Clearly when this novel was written, episodes such as these were truly adven-tures on the highroads.

The story then continues with d'Artagnan's encounter with the duke of Buckingham and the revelation of the duke's power. Since this novel is also a romantic novel, Dumas' emphasis is often on the power of love. D'Artagnan is in awe of the duke's willingness to use all of his power in the service of his beloved Anne of Austria, queen of France. However, we should remember that this adventure which d'Artagnan undertakes (during which he proves himself to be reso-lute, brave, and ingenious) is undertaken because of his own devoted love for Constance Bonacieux. Thus we have two plots of love and adventure: one centering on court intrigues; the other, on the romantic intrigues of a daring adventurer and his beloved.

Earlier in the novel, it seemed a superficial scene when d'Artagnan accosted Constance Bonacieux on the Pont-Neuf bridge while she was accompanying a disguised man. Then we learned that the man was the duke of Buckingham; now we can see that Dumas created this unlikely encounter in order for d'Artagnan—a common, foreign soldier—to get an interview with the most powerful man in England. He can identify himself now as "the young man who nearly fought you one night on the Pont-Neuf."

During the queen's encounter with the cardinal, concerning the diamond tags, the cardinal displays his brilliance in the way that he is able to "explain" his motives, but the queen is equally clever; she lets the cardinal know that she is aware of all his secret machinations against her.

These chapters also anticipate future chapters in that we hear more about Milady, a woman who will prove to be the very blackest quintessence of evil, a character responsible for the deaths of many people later in the novel. Likewise, Count de Wardes will also appear later, although in a lesser role than Milady.

Part 3

CHAPTERS 23–24

Summary

Arriving home, d'Artagnan learns from Planchet that a letter has mysteriously appeared. D'Artagnan anxiously opens the letter and discovers that Constance Bonacieux requests a rendezvous with him for ten o'clock that night. Ecstatic, he tells Planchet to meet him at seven that night with two horses (Note: at the end of the chapter, the two men meet at nine P.M. instead of seven, a minor slip by Dumas).

Leaving the apartment, d'Artagnan meets Monsieur Bonacieux, who questions him about his recent absence from Paris. D'Artagnan then contacts Monsieur de Tréville who, upon hearing about d'Artagnan's adventures in England, strongly advises d'Artagnan to sell the diamond ring which the queen gave him and leave Paris for awhile in order to avoid the cardinal's wrath: "The cardinal has a long memory and a powerful hand. He'll do something against you, you can be sure of that." D'Artagnan promises to leave the next day, but tonight he has other plans. Tréville is sure that a woman is involved.

At nine o'clock, d'Artagnan and Planchet wend their way toward the bungalow designated by Constance Bonacieux. Planchet complains of the cold and stops at an inn; meanwhile, d'Artagnan arrives at the bungalow. He waits until ten, then ten-thirty, and then he waits until eleven before climbing up a tree to look through a window. There, he discovers a room in total disarray. "Everything in the room bore witness to a violent, desperate struggle."

D'Artagnan awakens an old man who lives behind the bungalow, and after pleading with him, he softens the old man's sympathies and learns that three men came to his shack and borrowed a ladder. The old man saw a distinguished gentleman take a key and open the door to the bungalow. A woman screamed loudly and tried to climb out of the window, but her escape was blocked by two men on the ladder. They forcibly took the lady to a waiting carriage and left. After d'Artagnan listens to a description of the men, he is sure that one of them is "the man from Meung"; the other description fits the despicable Monsieur Bonacieux. However, he can do nothing until next morning, when Planchet arrives with the horses.

Commentary

In these chapters we move away from the world of adventure and into the world of romance and intrigue. When d'Artagnan reads Constance Bonacieux's letter, he is elated; no amount of personal danger can prevent him from keeping his rendezvous. Tréville warns him to leave Paris that very night, but d'Artagnan will not leave until his rendezvous with Constance Bonacieux, the woman for whom he completed the arduous and dangerous mission to London. D'Artagnan's elation is particularly evident when he impulsively and impetuously gives his servant, Planchet, an "ecu" (about $8.00, probably equal to more than two or three months' salary).

These two chapters continue to present Monsieur Bonacieux as a slimy, distasteful person. We first saw his spitefulness when he refused to go to London to aid the queen. Now we see something so despicable as his helping "the man from Meung" (actually, Count de Rochefort) kidnap Bonacieux's own wife, Constance. No doubt Dumas intended this scene to justify Constance's decision to have a romantic liaison with d'Artagnan.

These chapters also focus again on the immense power which the cardinal wields. Seemingly, Cardinal Richelieu is omnipresent and omniscient – a very dangerous combination. Dumas' precise characterization of Richelieu will justify d'Artagnan's later adventures – particularly when he realizes that he must leave Paris immediately and remain out of reach of the cardinal and his spies.

CHAPTERS 25–27

Summary

D'Artagnan decides to tell Tréville the entire story of Constance Bonacieux's abduction. Afterward, Tréville is certain that the entire matter was conceived by the cardinal. He tells d'Artagnan to leave Paris as soon as possible.

When d'Artagnan returns to his apartment, he is accosted by old Bonacieux, who tries to question him about his recent whereabouts. D'Artagnan notices the mud on Bonacieux's boots and is convinced that Bonacieux did indeed aid in kidnapping his own wife. Upstairs, Planchet tells d'Artagnan that the cardinal's captain of the guard, Monsieur de Cavois, stopped by to extend an invitation to d'Artagnan to visit the cardinal. Planchet wisely told the captain that d'Artagnan was out of town. They decide to leave immediately.

At the inn where they left Porthos, d'Artagnan orders some wine, which he shares with the innkeeper while discreetly trying to learn the whereabouts of Porthos. He learns that Porthos fought a duel and was seriously wounded, that he lost all of his money gambling, and that he has run up a large bill which he can't pay. In addition, Porthos gave the innkeeper a letter to be posted to Porthos' "duchess." The innkeeper ordered his servant to deliver the letter in person and discovered that the "duchess" was only Madame Coquenard – a plain, fiftyish, lawyer's wife.

When d'Artagnan goes to see Porthos, he pretends that he knows nothing about the dueling wound and listens attentively as Porthos fabricates a story about his tripping and hurting his knee. Obviously, he is being well cared for by his servant, Mousqueton, who knows all about poaching and getting wine by lassoing it through a small window. D'Artagnan bids farewell and tells Porthos that he will be back, about eight days later.

Lost in thought, d'Artagnan arrives at the inn in Crèvecoeur where they left Aramis. He is told by the congenial hostess that Aramis is still there—at present, entertaining the local curate and the superior of the local Jesuits. When d'Artagnan approaches, Aramis' servant tries to block the door; Bazin is anxious to serve a religious master, and he fears that d'Artagnan will lure Aramis away from his current religious meditations and commitments.

When d'Artagnan enters the room, he is stunned by the stark simplicity of the room—only religious objects are to be seen. Aramis tries to draw d'Artagnan into a ridiculously esoteric religious question concerning whether a priest should bless the congregation with one hand, with two hands, or with his fingers. After the priests leave, Aramis tells d'Artagnan that he has foresworn the world, that he hates all wordly ties, that his friends are but shadows, that love has no meaning to him, and that the world is a tomb.

Aramis then confesses to d'Artagnan that he was brought up in a seminary and that everyone fully expected that he would become a priest. When he was nineteen, however, while he was reading to a beautiful young lady, he was ordered out of the house and threatened by another guest, a young officer who was jealous of the attention which the young lady bestowed upon Aramis. Aramis left the seminary, took fencing lessons for a year, tracked down the officer, challenged him and killed him. Now he plans to return to the seminary.

Teasingly, d'Artagnan tells Aramis that if he is determined to return to a life of celibacy, he probably won't be interested in a perfumed letter that is sealed with a duchess' coronet and comes from the household of Madame de Chevreuse. Suddenly, Aramis has a change of heart. He grabs the letter, reads it, and becomes ecstatic. He embraces d'Artagnan—and all worldly matters. He can hardly wait to rejoin the musketeers. He tries to mount the magnificent horse that d'Artagnan brought him, but he is still too weak to ride, so d'Artagnan leaves him at the inn to practice riding until he is stronger.

D'Artagnan then rides on to find Athos, the musketeer for whom he has a special liking because Athos carries himself with such proud, noble grace and conducts himself with such aristocratic authority.

Remembering that the innkeeper accused Athos of trying to pass counterfeit money, d'Artagnan is filled with fresh indignation and anger when he arrives. The innkeeper begs to be listened to; he explains that he had been forewarned by the authorities that some men who fit the musketeers' descriptions were expected in the neighborhood and that they were criminals disguised as musketeers. He received a description of their uniforms, their servants, and their facial features. He tells d'Artagnan that Athos killed one of the men in the inn and seriously wounded two more; then he barricaded himself in the basement and threatened to kill anyone who tried to get near him. The innkeeper went to the police, but they wouldn't help him because the instructions concerning the fraudulent musketeers did not come from them. They refused to interfere and arrest someone who might be one of the King's Musketeers.

Athos remained in the basement, and now he has drunk over a hundred and fifty bottles of wine, he has eaten all the hams and sausages in the basement, and the innkeeper is almost financially ruined. Amends are finally made, however, and d'Artagnan and Athos leave Athos' old horse with the innkeeper to compensate his losses.

At supper that night, Athos becomes very drunk and tells d'Artagnan, who is bemoaning the fate of his beloved Constance Bonacieux, about his own misfortunes in love. Pretending that he is telling the story of "a young friend," he explains that this "friend" once met a beautiful sixteen-year-old girl, fell in love with her and married her; later, while the "friend" and his young wife were out riding, she fell and, while trying to help her regain consciousness, the "friend" loosened the upper part of her dress and discovered that she had been branded on the shoulder with a fleur-de-lis, a sign that she was a convicted criminal. Athos says that his "friend" immediately hanged his young wife.

Commentary

Essentially these three chapters serve to tell us more about each of the three musketeers. Chapter 25 gives us additional information about the vain Porthos, Chapter 26 shows us Aramis' conflict between love and religion, and Chapter 27 tells us more about Athos' past, which haunts him and drives him to excessive drinking.

While reading Chapter 25, we should remember that d'Artagnan first encountered Porthos when he collided with him on a stairwell and, by accident, it was revealed that Porthos was wearing a golden shoulder belt that was only half gilded. In that encounter, injured vanity was the principal reason why Porthos challenged d'Artagnan to a duel. Likewise, in this chapter, the emphasis is again on Porthos' extreme vanity. As noted in the summary, Porthos cannot admit that he was bested in a duel. Likewise, he feels that he needs to brag about his young and beautiful "duchess" when, in reality, his "duchess" is a fiftyish wife of a lawyer. Yet note that d'Artagnan, although a young man, is astute enough not to mention the truth to Porthos; he allows Porthos to continue with his fantasies.

Although Dumas revealed to us earlier that Monsieur Bonacieux assisted in his wife's abduction, it is only in Chapter 25 that d'Artagnan becomes fully aware of this fact. Remembering the description given to him of the fat little man, he looks at Bonacieux's shoes and realizes that he and Bonacieux have the same kind of red mud on their shoes. "At the same time he also noticed Bonacieux's shoes and stockings: they were spotted with exactly the same kind of mud. An idea flashed into his mind: that short, fat, gray-haired man, treated without respect by the noblemen who abducted Madame Bonacieux, was Bonacieux himself! The husband had taken part in his wife's abduction!" D'Artagnan concludes that Bonacieux is a miserable scoundrel.

Chapter 26 reveals the whereabouts of Aramis and focuses on the conflict between love and religion. As long as a person loves, and is loved in return, and knows the whereabouts of his beloved, religious matters rarely fill one with anguish. But if one feels rejected in love, as does Aramis, then a viable alternative to love in this world is a religious life in a monastery. That is, when Aramis thinks that he has been rejected, he turns to religion for solace.

However, when Aramis receives a letter from his beloved – Madame de Chevreuse, the friend of the queen whom the king suspected of connivance and banished to Tours – Aramis becomes ecstatic. He immediately disavows his religious plans and tells d'Artagnan that he is bursting with happiness. He rejects the religiously correct meal of spinach and eggs, and, instead, he orders meat, game, fowl, and the bottle of wine which he rejected only moments earlier. Here, in this typical romantic novel, the power of love once again triumphs.

While d'Artagnan is on his way to find Athos, he wonders why he feels closer to Athos than he does to the other two musketeers; clearly he and Athos are the furthest apart in age. He concludes that he is attracted to Athos because Athos seems so noble in his conduct, has such a distinguished air, and has such sudden flashes of grandeur.

Also, Athos' face suggests a striking sense of majesty combined with graciousness. At this point, d'Artagnan does not know that Athos is descended from nobility, but he can nevertheless recognize that Athos seems to have noble heritage. Later in the novel, d'Artagnan will not be too surprised when he learns about Athos' nobility.

Athos, however, does not always "act noble." Dumas continually characterizes him as a heavy drinker, and part of the humor in Chapter 27 is derived from Athos' barricading himself, by accident, in a *wine* cellar. Clearly, Athos does not suffer unduly during his two weeks there; we see that he survives on hams and sausages and consumes over one hundred and fifty bottles of wine. (His servant drinks only from the casks.)

Later, when Athos tells d'Artagnan a story about a young lord who once married a beautiful sixteen-year-old girl, he is, of course, telling his own story. But not until the last part of the novel will we discover that this beautiful girl is Milady, Lady de Winter – the evil nemesis to all of the loyalists. The only false part of Athos' story is his report that he hanged her and that she is dead. Foreshadowings such as this are virtual proof that Dumas had his novel well plotted and did not write, as some critics believe, without knowing where he was going next.

CHAPTERS 28–29

Summary

Next morning, Athos maintains that everything he told d'Artagnan the night before was only the ramblings of a drunken musketeer; there was no truth to any of it. He also confesses that when he got up that morning, he was somewhat muddle-headed and gambled away his magnificent horse. D'Artagnan is deeply disappointed. Then Athos reveals that he also gambled away d'Artagnan's horse as well. D'Artagnan believes that Athos has lost his mind. Then Athos further confesses that he gambled – and lost – the silver harnesses, saddles, and other elegant trappings.

D'Artagnan is speechless. Then comes the bitterest blow of all: Athos says that he gambled away d'Artagnan's diamond ring, the one which the queen gave him. D'Artagnan can only exclaim "My God" in total disbelief. Athos then says that he gambled for his servant, Grimaud – and won back the diamond ring, Then, using the ring, he

won back the harnesses. And then he quit. Now they have harnesses —
but no horses.

Athos convinces d'Artagnan that he should try a toss of the dice —
that he should at least *try* to win back his horse, or 100 pistoles. When
d'Artagnan wins, Athos talks him into accepting the 100 pistoles, rather
than the horse, because he will need the money to continue his search
for Constance Bonacieux. D'Artagnan agrees, and they set off on their
servants' old horses to meet Aramis.

Aramis confesses to his friends that he sold his magnificent
English horse to pay for some masses that he had earlier contracted
for, and now he has only the harness left. When they meet Porthos,
he asks them to sit down to a magnificent and extravagant meal. Shortly thereafter, Athos asks them to identify what they are eating, and
after one of them names an elegant dish, he tells them that they are
all eating, as it were, "horse." He realizes that Porthos had to sell his
horse in order to pay his debts and eat well. "But," Porthos explains,
"I saved the harness."

Arriving in Paris, they learn from Tréville that d'Artagnan has been
admitted to the King's Musketeers, but no date has been set for the
formal ceremony. They also learn that they *must* have their equipment ready in two weeks because they will be leaving for battle. At
present, none of them has enough money to buy equipment, and they
each need about 2000 livres each. Athos hopes that they can talk
d'Artagnan into selling his diamond ring.

While pondering how to get some money, d'Artagnan notes that
Porthos is curling his mustache; moments later, Porthos slips into a
church. D'Artagnan follows him and watches as Porthos goes quietly
up to a middle-aged woman (whom he intentionally ignores) and de-
liberately flirts with a beautiful and obviously wealthy lady at the front
of the church. D'Artagnan recognizes the beautiful lady as Milady,
the woman whom he saw at Meung. The middle-aged woman turns
out to be Madame Coquenard, the mistress whom Porthos wrote to
for money and who ignored his request. As d'Artagnan leaves, he
notices that Madame Coquenard is pleading with Porthos for forgive-
ness. He is fairly sure that Porthos will get his musketeer supplies
and a horse.

Commentary

D'Artagnan was rewarded so richly with the magnificent horses for his friends that he is deeply hurt when he learns that the horses have been sold. He is additionally horrified to learn that Athos dared to gamble with d'Artagnan's diamond ring. But we should remember that d'Artagnan took a great deal for granted when he told the three musketeer friends that they were going to accompany him on his trip to London – that is, they all risked their lives for him without even knowing or questioning why he demanded such dedication from them. Now they have all sold or lost their horses, even though they have the harnesses. This fact is fortunate because in Chapter 29, they learn that they must have full equipment ready in two weeks, and their harnesses are one less thing that they will have to buy.

Chapter 29 also includes mention of Milady, or as we come to know her, Lady de Winter, the person who snipped the diamond tags from Buckingham's suit so that the cardinal could try to entrap the queen. As d'Artagnan increasingly begins to follow her, the novel will frequently focus on her influence over him. Similarly, we see that Porthos has successfully established himself in Madame Coquenard's affections.

CHAPTERS 30–33

Summary

D'Artagnan follows Milady and hears her tell the coachman to go to Saint-Germain, a neighborhood too distant for him to follow on foot. Therefore, he decides to visit Athos; he tells him about Milady, but Athos is not sympathetic. Athos is cynical about all love affairs; he sarcastically tells d'Artagnan, "Go have an adventure with Milady. I wish you success with all of my heart."

D'Artagnan finds Planchet, they borrow two horses from Tréville, and ride to Saint-Germain. There, Planchet sees a man whom he recognizes: the servant to Count de Wardes – the same servant whom Planchet fought outside Calais. D'Artagnan sends Planchet to the servant to see if Planchet will be recognized, and if he isn't, to find out if the count survived. After talking with Planchet for awhile, the count's servant leaves, and suddenly Milady's maid appears. She gives Planchet a note intended for the servant of Count de Wardes. The maid says, "For your master." Planchet takes the piece of paper to d'Artagnan, and they discover that it is a love note: Milady is asking the count for a rendezvous.

Later, while he is following Milady's carriage, d'Artagnan overhears Milady in a heated argument with a man. Impulsively, d'Artagnan comes to her rescue, but is told by Milady that she is not in danger; she is only arguing with her brother-in-law. After she leaves, the two men agree to a duel, along with a free-for-all with three friends to be brought by each duelist. The gentleman introduces himself as Lord de Winter. D'Artagnan returns home and tells the three musketeers that he has committed them to a duel. All three are excited at the prospect.

Before the duel, the Englishmen are clearly concerned that they are titled members of society and perhaps should not be fighting with mere "commoners." Therefore, Athos takes one of them aside and tells him who he really is. He also tells him that because he now knows Athos' true identity, Athos will have to kill him — and he does so only moments into the duel. Meanwhile, Porthos wounds his opponent in the thigh, picks him up, and carries him to the carriage. Aramis traps his opponent momentarily before the Englishman manages to escape. D'Artagnan fights Lord de Winter with cool detachment until he is able to unarm him; then graciously, he spares his life. In appreciation, de Winter arranges to introduce d'Artagnan to Milady, his sister-in-law, Lady de Winter.

When the two men arrive, Milady seems momentarily unhappy to learn that d'Artagnan spared de Winter's life, but quickly recovers her composure. She becomes gracious to d'Artagnan, and soon d'Artagnan becomes a daily visitor to Milady's house.

Meanwhile, Porthos goes to his dinner engagement with Madame Coquenard, posing as her cousin. Her miserly husband is there, and their dinner is the poorest excuse of a meal that Porthos, a fastidious gourmet, has ever tried to eat. In addition, he is served the most foul-tasting wine that can be imagined. After the meal, he discovers that Madame Coquenard is as miserly as her husband; she almost faints when she hears how much money Porthos needs to buy new musketeer equipment for himself. Nonetheless, she promises to get most of the equipment (a horse, a mule, and some other things) from business acquaintances, and she further promises Porthos some money. Disappointed, hungry, and morose, Porthos goes home.

Hourly, d'Artagnan is falling more in love with Milady. He is not even aware that the lady's exceptionally pretty maid, Kitty, takes every opportunity to rub against him. Finally one day, Kitty takes d'Artagnan aside and tells him that her mistress does not love him. D'Artagnan, being young and ardent, does not believe Kitty, so she takes him up to her private room, next to her mistress' chamber. There, she gives d'Artagnan a note that Milady has written to Count de Wardes. D'Artagnan reads the note, an open plea for the count to take advantage of Milady's love for him.

After reading the note, d'Artagnan pleads with Kitty to help him take revenge on Milady, but Kitty refuses; she says that in matters of love, it's "everyone for herself." Just then, d'Artagnan recalls Kitty's languishing glances, her flirtatious greetings in the antechamber, the corridor, and on the stairs, those touches of the hand every time she meets him, and her deep, warm sighs. D'Artagnan is shrewd enough to realize how advantageous it would be to have Kitty as a mistress; therefore, for the rest of the evening, he turns his attentions to her.

When Milady calls to Kitty, d'Artagnan hides in a closet where he can overhear their conversation. He learns that Milady knows that d'Artagnan has foiled her plots; she says that she detests him, that he is a simple country fool, and that she hates him most for not killing Lord de Winter, her brother-in-law. Had d'Artagnan killed de Winter, Milady would have inherited an extremely large fortune. D'Artagnan realizes that Milady is utterly corrupt, a monster.

Because d'Artagnan has won Kitty's love, she is eager to please him, so she brings him another letter that Milady has written to Count de Wardes. D'Artagnan forges an answer, setting up a rendezvous for 11 P.M., and signs the count's name. Kitty fears the consequences, and she doesn't want to deliver the letter, but she is finally persuaded to — especially after he reminds her what vengeance Milady would take against her if she ever found out about Kitty's betrayals.

Commentary

When Athos tells d'Artagnan to go and amuse himself with Milady, little does Athos realize that he is telling d'Artagnan to amuse himself with the woman whom he once married — the woman whom he believes he murdered. This coincidence is, of course, one of the romantic ironies of this loose and seemingly rambling novel, but a novel which is nevertheless well-plotted. One would have thought that d'Artagnan would have recognized the name "Lord de Winter" since he had heard from Buckingham that it was "Lady de Winter" who cut off the diamond tags – but Dumas explains this puzzling detail by having d'Artagnan admit that de Winter's English name is so strange-sounding that he can't even pronounce it. Ultimately, all of these unlikely coincidences – that is, the accidental sighting in the church, the inadvertent interception of Milady's note to Count de Wardes, the duel with Milady's brother-in-law, and d'Artagnan's sparing his life – prepare us for the actual introduction of d'Artagnan to the beautiful Lady de Winter herself, the infamous Milady.

Chapter 31 presents another exciting duel scene, the type of scene that makes this novel a favorite of Hollywood filmmakers. Here, it is worth noting that the only Englishman killed is Athos' opponent; Athos, remember, confided his real name and social status to the Englishman. Athos' secret is so personal at this point in the novel that it is necessary that Athos kill the Englishman to make sure that his secret will not be revealed. Thus, for the present, Athos' real identity continues to be a secret, and his origins and background become even more intriguing.

Chapter 32 presents an entertaining interlude. It is an established comic device to pit an extreme miser (Madame Coquenard) against an extreme libertine and spendthrift (Porthos). We have continually seen that Porthos puts great emphasis on fine and delicate foods prepared to perfection. In earlier chapters, Porthos was the one who suggested spending money on good meals. Earlier too, he sold his beautiful English horse so that he could enjoy an elegant repast. Therefore, when we now see the finicky Porthos being subjected to watery soup, the wing of a scrawny chicken, inedible green beans, undrinkable wine, and a dessert that clogs the throat – all for the sake of getting Madame Coquenard to provide new musketeer equipment – this is an extremely comic situation from an author who is not particularly known for his comic touch. Dumas even satirically compares Madame Coquenard to Moliere's famous character Harpagon in *The Miser*, but points out that Madame Coquenard lived many years before Moliere created his now-archetypal skinflint.

In Chapter 33, Dumas begins building suspense for one of the novel's most significant intrigues. We know that d'Artagnan has a great deal of pride and ambition, so it is not surprising that he realizes that Kitty is an exceptionally pretty mistress who can satisfy his immediate needs and whom he can use to revenge himself on Milady. This reasoning is prudent because without Kitty's help, d'Artagnan could never effect his long-range plans. He desperately lusts for Milady – even though he knows of her hatred for him – and yet, at the same time, he is desperate for revenge. He knows what a monster Milady is, but he cannot rid himself of his passionate desire to possess her: "He knew her to be treacherous in matters of more importance, and he had no respect for her, yet he felt an uncontrollable passion for this woman boiling in his veins – passion drunk with contempt but passion and desire nevertheless." Throughout d'Artagnan's relationship with Milady, we should be aware of Dumas' use of the modern-day love/hate dichotomy.

CHAPTERS 34–38

Summary

Next day, d'Artagnan visits the three musketeers in Athos' apartment and finds them all in vastly different moods. Mousqueton arrives and tells Porthos to return home for a very important matter. Then Bazin comes in and tells Aramis that there is a beggar from Tours waiting to talk to him (Tours, remember, is the town where Aramis' beloved Madame de Chevreuse lives in exile). Both Porthos and Aramis leave immediately. Alone with Athos, d'Artagnan tells him about the romantic escapades with Milady.

Meanwhile, Aramis arrives home, and the beggar gives him a letter which says, "It is the will of fate that we should still be separated for some time, but the wonderful and happy days of youth are not lost beyond recall." Madame de Chevreuse has sent money by the beggar, who is really a Spanish nobleman in disguise. Thus, Aramis now has enough money to buy first-rate musketeer equipment, and he also has enough money to buy his friends a splendid dinner.

Athos, however, still refuses to leave his apartment; he says that he will have his dinner sent up. D'Artagnan, on his way to see Porthos, notices Porthos' servant leading an old nag and a disreputable mule. D'Artagnan recognizes the nag as the one which his father gave him, the one which he sold for three ecus. He is told that Porthos' mistress' husband is responsible for the insult and that Porthos is sending the animals back to be tied to the Coquenards' front door.

Later, Porthos confronts Madame Coquenard, and using his most disdainful, lordly, and aristocratic manner, he orders her to meet him later, letting her know the utter contempt he has for such a disgraceful horse. Madame Coquenard promises to make amends if Porthos will come to her house when her husband is gone. Porthos now feels certain that she will soon open her secret treasure chest and he will have a chance to view all of its fabulous contents.

Early in the evening, d'Artagnan visits Milady and immediately notices that she is impatient; he knows that she is anxious for him to be gone so that she can (she thinks) receive Count de Wardes. D'Artagnan leaves and goes to Kitty's room, where he waits for the hour assigned for Count de Wardes' visit. The only way he can console Kitty is to keep reminding her that he is acting solely out of his desire for revenge. Later, he hears Milady wildly delirious with happiness, instructing Kitty to make sure that all of the lights are out when the count arrives.

When it is dark within, d'Artagnan enters Milady's room. She presses his hand and asks for a token of love from him tomorrow. As proof of her own love for him tonight, she gives him a magnificent sapphire ring surrounded by diamonds, a ring that she suggests is a relief to be rid of. He then hears her refer to himself, d'Artagnan, as "that Gascon monster"; she vows to revenge herself against him. When d'Artagnan hears himself referred to with such derogatory names, he realizes the hate and contempt that she has for him; yet this woman has an "incredible power" over him. He hates and adores her at the same time.

Next morning, wearing the sapphire ring, d'Artagnan visits Athos. Athos examines the ring and turns pale. He is certain that he recognizes the ring; it is exactly like the one which once belonged to his family, the ring which he gave to his wife during a night of love. Finding a unique scratch on one of the stone's facets, Athos is certain that it is the same ring. Yet it is a mystery how Milady, Lady de Winter, happened to have this ring.

When d'Artagnan arrives home, Kitty is waiting for him with a note to de Wardes; Milady is asking de Wardes to come back sooner than he said he would. D'Artagnan begins plotting his revenge. He writes a note to Milady, stating that he ("de Wardes") is involved with other mistresses and that she (Milady) will have to wait her "turn." He signs the note, "Count de Wardes." When Milady reads the note, she vows revenge against de Wardes.

For two days, d'Artagnan stays away from Milady; on the third day, Milady sends Kitty with a note asking d'Artagnan to call. That night, he goes to her house and instantly he notices that her face seems ravaged with torment. Even though he knows that she is a wicked woman who casts evil, hypnotic spells on men, d'Artagnan finds himself once again under her spell. He believed that his love for her was extinguished, but now he knows that it was only smoldering. Now he feels as if he would risk damnation for her smile. Milady, knowing that he loves her, asks if he will do something for her, and d'Artagnan promises that he will do anything for her.

Milady says that she has an enemy ("a mortal enemy") – but just as she is about to speak the enemy's name, d'Artagnan speaks it for her. When she inquires how he knows the man's name, he lies to her. He says that de Wardes was bragging about his seductive success with Milady and showing everyone the ring that she gave him. This revelation incenses Milady, but since d'Artagnan is going to kill de Wardes in a duel, she promises d'Artagnan sexual satisfaction that evening at eleven.

Milady's kisses are as cold as stone, but d'Artagnan is nonetheless passionately and blindly in love with her. His youth, his pride, his vanity, and his mad passion make him believe that Milady loves him. Later, after they have made love for two hours, Milady wants to discuss her revenge against de Wardes. At this point, d'Artagnan reveals that it was *he* and *not de Wardes* who made love to her in the dark last week, and that it is *he* who has the valuable ring.

D'Artagnan has never seen such violent hatred in a woman as that which erupts within Milady. She attacks him and during a struggle, her negligee is torn, revealing a fleur-de-lis, the mark of a convicted criminal, indelibly branded on one of her smooth white shoulders. Milady has only one thought: "Now he knew her secret, her terrible secret that no one else knew." Knowing that d'Artagnan must be killed, Milady attacks the half-naked youth with a knife. D'Artagnan is terror-stricken at Milady's face, now contorted by hatred, fury, and revenge; her lips are blood-red and her pupils are horribly dilated. Suddenly Kitty opens the door and d'Artagnan is able to escape – after quickly slipping into women's clothes.

Despite the fact that d'Artagnan is wearing a woman's dress, he goes immediately to Athos' house, where he tells Athos that Milady has a fleur-de-lis branded on one of her shoulders – just like Athos' late wife, the woman whom Athos believes he hanged. Comparing notes, the two men realize that Milady and Athos' wife are the same person. Athos knows how evil and dangerous Milady can be, and he warns d'Artagnan.

They send Grimaud to ask Planchet to bring clothing for d'Artagnan, and meanwhile, d'Artagnan tries to give Athos the diamond and sapphire ring which rightfully belongs to him. Athos, however, will not take back his mother's ring because it has been sullied by Milady. He can't bring himself to sell it, so he asks d'Artagnan to pawn it so that they can split the money. D'Artagnan tries to refuse his half of the money, but Athos tells him that he must accept half of the money or he, Athos, will throw the ring in the river. Hearing this threat, d'Artagnan agrees to take it.

Kitty enters, begging for help. By now, Milady is sure to know that Kitty is d'Artagnan's accomplice, and Kitty is convinced that her life is in danger. D'Artagnan recalls Aramis' friend in Tours and asks him to write a letter to this noble woman, asking her to protect Kitty. Aramis agrees and hands Kitty a sealed letter for the mysterious lady in Tours.

The ring is pawned, and they buy equipment for Athos; Athos, however, realizes that he never wants to see the ring again, so he tells d'Artagnan to go back and get two hundred more ecus for the ring and sell it outright. Now Athos has his equipment—and money to spare.

Commentary

These chapters include some of the most exciting intrigues in the entire novel. They are compellingly narrated, demonstrating Dumas' genius as a storyteller.

Chapter 34 is constructed like an interlude, showing how Aramis receives a mysterious letter delivered by a beggar who demands that Aramis show proof of identification. It turns out that the beggar is really a Spanish nobleman. Remember that the queen (Anne of Austria) is Spanish and that her closest friend, Madame de Chevreuse, has been exiled to Tours; since the Spanish noblemen are enemies of France, we must assume that the beggar is also a close friend of the queen and Madame de Chevreuse. Aramis is ecstatic over the letter and declares his love for her. Once again, love and intrigue are inextricably intertwined in this novel.

Meanwhile, love has also entangled the usually placid Porthos. He has "used" love to threaten his mistress who, in her miserliness, tried to give Porthos an ugly nag, the one that belonged to d'Artagnan when he first came to Paris. Finally, however, her infatuation, devotion, and love for Porthos makes her relent and, through the power of love, both Aramis and Porthos obtain their military equipment, even though the means are quite different.

D'Artagnan's entanglement with love is also comic – even if his life is at stake. Before de Wardes is due to rendezvous with Milady, she insists that all of the lights be out. This might seem like an amateurish way for Dumas to have d'Artagnan accomplish his deception, but ultimately, Dumas is creating this scene exactly as a shrewd woman might prepare for a rendezvous. Milady wants the room darkened so that her lover will not be able to see that she has a fleur-de-lis branded on one of her shoulders; she musn't allow anyone to know that she is a branded, convicted criminal. Only later, when Milady and d'Artagnan make love until daylight and he accidentally tears her gown, is her dreadful secret exposed. Furiously, she vows to kill d'Artagnan – primarily so that she can protect her dreadful secret. Most men would not be so obsessed with such a wicked woman, but d'Artagnan is entrapped in a typical love/hate dichotomy wherein he is so strongly attracted to Milady's physical beauty that he cannot face the reality of her corruption. He is a very young man, and he wants Milady to love him for himself. He is sure that he is more handsome than de Wardes – he has a better body, he is stronger, prouder, and he is a better swordsman. In his youth and vanity, d'Artagnan cannot believe that Milady would really prefer someone else.

In Chapter 35, when Athos realizes that the sapphire ring with the diamond facets is the same one that he gave to his late wife (don't forget that he thinks he hanged her), he can surmise only that either she sold the ring or that, somehow, Milady gained possession of it. At this point, it does not occur to him that Milady is his wife. It is only after d'Artagnan describes her and the fleur-de-lis branded on her shoulder that Athos realizes that this evil, wicked woman is the same evil woman whom he cast aside long ago.

CHAPTERS 39–40

Summary

Planchet brings d'Artagnan two letters, a small one in a simple envelope and a large, imposing one with the cardinal's coat-of-arms on it. The small letter, although unsigned, is from Constance Bonacieux, instructing him to be on a certain road at 7 P.M. The other letter instructs d'Artagnan to be at the cardinal's palace at 8 P.M. D'Artagnan arranges for his three friends to be posted outside the cardinal's house, and then he purchases one of Aramis' elegant horses that was "mysteriously" sent to him by an unknown benefactoress and rides out to keep the seven o'clock appointment with Constance Bonacieux. Fleetingly, Constance appears at the window of a heavily guarded carriage; she throws him a kiss and gives him a sign not to acknowledge her.

D'Artagnan then returns in time for his eight o'clock appointment with the cardinal. At the beginning of the interview, the cardinal demonstrates that he knows many things about d'Artagnan—for example, he knows about d'Artagnan's first encounter with "the man from Meung," his losing the letter of introduction to Tréville, his trip to England, his meeting with the duke of Buckingham, and his meeting with the queen and her gift of the diamond ring. The cardinal assures d'Artagnan that he respects him highly, and he then offers him a position as lieutenant in his own guards—a very distinguished post. He also lets d'Artagnan know that he is aware of d'Artagnan's nocturnal activities, and he suggests that d'Artagnan needs protection from ladies who love him. He cautions d'Artagnan that if he were in the cardinal's service, he would have that protection. D'Artagnan refuses the offer because all of his friends are musketeers; he feels that he couldn't fit in with members of the cardinal's guards. The cardinal warns d'Artagnan that if something unfortunate should happen to him, it won't be the cardinal's fault. However, the cardinal does promise d'Artagnan that, for the time being, his feelings toward him are neutral; he is waiting to see how d'Artagnan conducts himself during the siege of La Rochelle.

Next day, during the inspection of the troops, all of the musketeers are magnificent in their new trappings. In fact, d'Artagnan is so concerned with his own appearance that he does not see Milady pointing him out to some sinister-looking, low-class rogues.

Commentary

In Chapter 39, d'Artagnan believes that Constance Bonacieux is still in captivity because she will not acknowledge him and his actions; later, however, we discover that she is being secretly transported according to the instructions of the queen to a rural convent for her protection.

Chapter 40 gives us one of the few favorable views of the cardinal. This is also the scene of the long-awaited meeting between d'Artagnan and the cardinal, and we are anxious to see how d'Artagnan conducts himself during the confrontation. Historically, Cardinal Richelieu was a superb diplomat, one of the most powerful men of his era; today, his name is far more famous than that of his king, Louis XIII.

In this scene, we see that the cardinal is fair; he respects virtue and loyalty, and he acknowledges d'Artagnan's superior qualities by offering him a promotion in the guards. Earlier, this offer would have been an undreamed-of opportunity for a young man from Gascony, but now d'Artagnan has formed his own allegiances. He refuses the cardinal's offer with a subtle and effectively diplomatic answer, proof that he has learned a great deal during his short stay in Paris. The cardinal's promise to be neutral, that he won't personally persecute or hound d'Artagnan, gives us a fuller perspective of Cardinal Richelieu. We are being prepared for d'Artagnan's ultimate alignment with the cardinal at the end of the novel.

Part 4

CHAPTERS 41–42

Summary

The siege of La Rochelle allows the cardinal an opportunity to fulfill two aims. First, he wants to rid France of its enemies, and second, he wants to take vengeance on a rival. That is, the cardinal was once in love with the queen, Anne of Austria, but she rejected him and accepted the romantic overtures of the duke of Buckingham, who is now declaring war on France, hoping to return triumphantly to Paris and rendezvous with the queen.

Since the king has a fever and cannot go to the battlefront, the musketeers are forced to remain behind with him. Thus, for the first time, d'Artagnan is separated from his friends. Since he has made no friends among the guards of his own division, he is out walking alone on an isolated road at twilight when he suddenly sees the end of a musket on one side of the road and another musket on the other side. He quickly and instinctively takes cover when both muskets are fired at him and he manages to escape before the ambushers can reload. He ponders the meaning of the attack and rejects the idea that it was the enemy who fired on him because the muskets were not military weapons. D'Artagnan cannot fathom the cardinal's stooping to ambush; finally, he decides that Milady was involved.

Two days later, Monsieur des Essarts, commander of the guard, informs d'Artagnan that the commander-in-chief is going to call for volunteers for a dangerous mission. D'Artagnan volunteers and, not surprisingly, he is made leader of the expedition. Two other officers and two ordinary soldiers also volunteer. The mission is to discover whether the enemy, on recapturing a bastion, left it guarded or unguarded. They will have to get dangerously close to the bastion. When they are approaching it, a volley of shots rings out, wounding one of the officers. Then two more shots ring out, and d'Artagnan is very nearly killed. He realizes instantly that the shots did *not* come from the enemy but that they came from *behind* him. He also realizes that the two common soldiers are trying to kill him and make it seem as though the enemy killed him. In fact, d'Artagnan believes, the two traitorous soldiers are the same two men who tried to ambush him earlier; he is absolutely certain that Milady conceived this plot.

D'Artagnan attacks and disarms the two soldiers. One of them manages to escape toward the bastion, but is shot by the enemy. The other soldier begs for mercy and confesses that they were indeed hired by Milady and that the wounded soldier has a letter from her. The letter chides the two soldiers for allowing Constance Bonacieux to escape and warns them *not* to allow d'Artagnan to escape.

Even though the letter isn't signed, d'Artagnan knows that it is from Milady, and he realizes anew what a terrible craving for revenge she has. Back at camp, he is accorded the reception of a hero, and his exploits are extolled by the entire command.

One morning in early November, d'Artagnan receives a letter telling him that the three musketeers are confined to quarters because of rowdy behavior, but that they have sent him twelve bottles of Anjou wine. D'Artagnan offers to share the wine with one of the guards, but just as they are about to drink up, a commotion announces the arrival of the king and the cardinal, and also – the three musketeers.

D'Artagnan thanks his friends for the wine and asks them to join him in drinking it. The musketeers tell him that *they* didn't send the wine, and all four of them simultaneously realize that Milady is responsible for the gift. At that moment, one of the guards who drank some of the wine falls down, poisoned. The four friends realize again that Milady is a worse threat than the enemy, and they decide to try to do something about her. D'Artagnan tells them that Constance Bonacieux is in a convent somewhere, but he doesn't know where. Aramis assures him that he will find the woman soon.

Commentary

These two chapters reveal to the reader what a powerful enemy d'Artagnan made when he saw the branded fleur-de-lis on Milady's naked shoulder. The extent of her drive for revenge is enormous. Three separate attempts on d'Artagnan's life have been made, and it is only because of d'Artagnan's alertness and daring during the first two attempts, and purely by accident during the incident of the Anjou wine that he is still alive. Even though these attemps to kill d'Artagnan are foiled, we will see in future chapters that Milady will never give up. She has vowed to see d'Artagnan dead – or die trying.

The beginning of Chapter 41 again emphasizes that the cardinal's persecution of the French queen is partly a result of jealousy: the queen prefers Buckingham to the cardinal. Dumas is insistent that the cardinal not be seen as merely a clever manipulator of people, but as a three-dimensional man, one spurned by the queen of France.

It is also worth noting that the separation of d'Artagnan from his friends sets the stage for several attempts on his life. Since his only close friends until now have been the three musketeers, it is believable that he would go for solitary walks. Were his three friends with him, d'Artagnan would never have been attacked by two cowardly dastards. However, because he is alone, he is attacked. Similarly, because he is alone and bored and eager to put some adventure into his life, he volunteers for a dangerous mission. D'Artagnan is continually trying to establish his own sense of identity and display leadership qualities – apart and separate from the three musketeers.

Lest someone think that d'Artagnan would not likely know that the unsigned letter in the wounded solder's uniform was from Milady, remember that he is familiar with Milady's handwriting. He has received love notes from her and, because of Kitty, he has been able to intercept love notes which she wrote to Count de Wardes. Dumas ties up most of his complicated plot elements very neatly and effectively.

CHAPTERS 43–45

Summary

The three musketeers have little to do because they are not yet involved in the siege, so they ride out to a neighboring inn. On the way back, they challenge an approaching rider who, in turn, challenges them with a voice of absolute authority. It is the cardinal. Surprisingly, he knows the names of each of the three musketeers; because his mission is secret, he asks them to accompany him in order that his safety be guaranteed. He knows their reputations for bravery, loyalty, and trustworthiness.

They learn that he is going to the inn which they just left, and they tell him about some rogues who tried to break into a lady's room. The musketeers were obliged to disperse these unsavory characters. The cardinal is pleased; the lady is the very person whom he is to meet. He asks the musketeers to wait for him in a room below while he goes up to talk to the lady.

In the musketeers' room, there is a broken stovepipe and, by accident, Athos discovers that he can hear the conversation between the cardinal and Milady. Porthos and Aramis also draw up their chairs and listen. They hear the cardinal tell Milady that she is to go to London to contact Buckingham and let him know that as soon as he attacks France, the cardinal will bring about the queen's ruin. Milady is also to tell Buckingham that the cardinal knows about his activities with the queen, and he describes each meeting which the duke has had with the queen, including a description of the clothes that the duke wore on each occasion. The cardinal also knows the truth about the diamond tags.

Furthermore, the cardinal's men have intercepted an Englishman who had letters on him (one from Madame de Chevreuse, Aramis' beloved) which compromise the queen because they prove that the queen is capable of loving the king's enemies and of conspiring with the enemies of France – charges which could imprison the queen for life. The cardinal is aware that the duke will do almost anything to protect the queen, but if the duke refuses, the cardinal indicates to Milady that she is to kill him – and make it look like the work of a fanatic. Milady agrees and, in return, she requests that *her* enemies be killed – first, Constance Bonacieux; and then, and even more important, she wants d'Artagnan killed. She will provide evidence that d'Artagnan has been in collusion with Buckingham; afterward, the cardinal will see to it that d'Artagnan disappears forever. Then she asks for, and receives, a valuable letter from the cardinal stating that whatever the bearer of the letter does, that person is doing so for the benefit of the cardinal and for France.

After hearing this, Athos makes ready to leave. He tells Aramis and Porthos to tell the cardinal that he has gone forward to scout the road – just in case there are unknown dangers. After the cardinal and the two remaining musketeers have left the inn, Athos returns to Milady's room and confronts her. She is horrified when she realizes that Athos is Count de La Fère, her husband, the man who tried to hang her and left her for dead.

Athos charges her with all of the vile, infamous things she has done and reviews her recent vengeful actions. Milady is stunned by his minutely detailed knowledge of her evil machinations, and Athos threatens her life if she doesn't cease trying to kill d'Artagnan. Milady defies Athos and vows that d'Artagnan will certainly die after she has made certain that Constance Bonacieux is dead. Athos draws his pistol and is about to kill her, but instead, he takes the letter which the cardinal wrote for her, and leaves.

Commentary

In these chapters, we have an ambiguous view of the cardinal. His request to the three musketeers, his acknowledgment that they are loyal and brave men, and his affirmation of the trust he has in them indicate that he is a man who recognizes good qualities in others. However, when the cardinal learns from Milady that d'Artagnan has been in collusion with Buckingham, he is determined to make sure that d'Artagnan is punished.

In Chapter 44, the device of having the three musketeers overhear the conversation between the cardinal and Milady is an easy, often-used fictional gimmick that good writers rarely use. In the romantic fiction of the nineteenth century, however, it was a favorite device. Sometimes a person hid behind a screen in the same room, or behind a shrub outside, or listened through a broken stovepipe, as we see here. (Actually, this "stovepipe device" is an anachronism on Dumas' part because the time period for the novel is the 1620s, and the stovepipe was not invented until the 1760s, by Benjamin Franklin in America. Dumas' novel was written in 1843–44, when the stovepipe was an established feature of many households.)

While the cardinal is giving Milady instructions, we are once again aware of how all-powerful and omniscient he is. He reveals that he knows almost every movement which the duke has ever made in France, including the duke's role in the intricate misadventures of the diamond tags. The cardinal is a shrewd diplomat; he knows that the duke will go to almost any length to protect Anne of Austria, the queen of France, and since there is an allegiance between England, Spain, Austria, and Lorraine against France, he must take drastic measures to assure France's safety and protect her powers. His ability to find the right methods to accomplish these things is what makes him such a powerful and feared man.

In Chapter 45, we learn Athos' real name – Count de La Fère – and we should recall that in the preface, Dumas wrote that he found a manuscript by Count de La Fère that recounts the events of this novel. During Athos' confrontation with Milady (alias Anne de Breuil, alias Countess de La Fère, alias Lady de Winter), he is stunned at the depths of her evil nature, her vile soul, and her infamous behavior. He thought he had killed her once and although he is on the verge of killing her now, he relents. He merely takes away her valuable "letter of protection," a letter which d'Artagnan will put to profitable use later on in the novel.

CHAPTERS 46–48

Summary

When the three musketeers meet d'Artagnan, they want to go someplace where they cannot be overhead as they make plans. They decide on an inn, but have no privacy there; they are continually bombarded with questions about d'Artagnan's exploits. When they hear some soldiers talking about a bastion that the enemy has taken and temporarily abandoned, Athos makes a bet that they can eat their breakfast there and remain safely in the bastion for one hour. The other soldiers bet against him.

Initially, d'Artagnan, Porthos, and Aramis are perplexed about Athos' ridiculous bet, but are reminded that they need privacy to discuss some very important matters that must remain absolutely secret. In the bastion, they will have complete privacy. Porthos wishes that they had remembered to bring their muskets, but Athos reminds them that when the bastion was stormed, twelve men and their muskets and powder were left lying there. They can use these weapons and receive even greater glory when their colleagues realize what a dangerous mission they went on, theoretically armed only with swords.

In Chapter 47, they enter the bastion, and Athos announces that he saw Milady the previous night. While d'Artagnan is registering surprise, Athos explains to the others what a wicked and evil woman she is and that she tried to have d'Artagnan shot and poisoned during the last two weeks.

Suddenly the musketeers see four soldiers and sixteen workmen approaching. Using the twelve muskets, they take careful aim, killing some of the soldiers and wounding the rest. The workmen flee. Resuming their talk, the musketeers and d'Artagnan decide that they must warn Buckingham against Milady's treachery, but since they are officially at war with England, they decide to warn Lord de Winter and tell him that he is about to be killed by his sister-in-law and that he should protect himself and Buckingham as well. Their next goal will be discovering the whereabouts of Madame Bonacieux before Milady and the cardinal do. Athos shows them the cardinal's "protection letter" which he took from Milady, signed by the cardinal and insuring absolute protection and permission to the bearer of the note. They decide to send Planchet to London and Bazin to Aramis' countess, but unfortunately, they realize, they need money to carry out their plans.

Grimaud abruptly announces that about twenty-five men are approaching. Athos has Grimaud place all the dead bodies outside and put muskets in their hands. Meanwhile, they finish their breakfast and see that they have probably ten more minutes before they can win their bet. They conceal themselves and carefully take aim at the approaching soldiers, kill several of them, and then, as the rest try to approach the bastion, they push over a rotting wall on them – killing or drowning most of them in the moat. Then they return gloriously to camp.

On the way, they wonder how they will get some money – and at this point they remember d'Artagnan's diamond ring. They convince him that since the queen gave it to him, it would be an honor to the queen if he were to sell it to help Buckingham, the queen's lover, and the money could also help rescue Constance Bonacieux, the queen's loyal servant.

They persuade Aramis to write a letter to de Winter and one to Madame de Chevreuse, using elegant, arabesque phrases so if the letter is confiscated or captured, the enemy (or the cardinal) will not understand the contents. Then they send Planchet and Bazin on the important errands, promising them extra money if they return at a specifically designated time. D'Artagnan has now been officially declared a musketeer, so the *four* musketeers while away their time, waiting for the servants to return. Not long afterward, both servants return on the designated day at the designated time.

Commentary

The episode in the bastion does little to advance the plot, but it does emphasize the daring and inventive bravado of the musketeers and d'Artagnan. Of course, the purpose of their going to the bastion, apart from its being a daring excursion, is to find a place where they can discuss secret strategy without being overheard. We know that the cardinal has spies in every nook and cranny of France – if not in all of Europe – therefore, only in a captured and temporarily abandoned bastion can they find sufficient privacy to make plans to thwart Milady's scheme to kill Constance Bonacieux and d'Artagnan.

Athos is characterized in this episode as a true leader: he knows that the muskets belonging to the dead soldiers are still beside their bodies, and by placing the dead men and their muskets on the bastion's parapet, he shows great ingenuity: the attacking soldiers will be firing at dead bodies while the musketeers will be taking direct aim at the attacking soldiers.

Once again, during their discussion about Milady, we realize that she is one of the most villainous and crafty women imaginable. She is totally amoral; she will sacrifice anyone to her deadly, vengeful schemes.

It is interesting to see how several earlier adventures prepared the way for these present adventures. For example, if Planchet had not accompanied d'Artagnan on the trip to England, he would not know how to get there now. Likewise, because Bazin is known by Madame de Chevreuse as Aramis' servant, he will be recognized and trusted.

CHAPTERS 49–51

Summary

Milady's ship is detained by a storm, and when she finally reaches England, Planchet has already warned de Winter of Milady's wicked plans; meanwhile, Planchet is now boarding a ship heading back to France. Therefore, when Milady's ship docks, she is received by an austere English officer who, with utmost politeness, escorts her to a castle some distance away and places her in a locked room. Milady is livid with anger and indignation, but after awhile, Lord de Winter appears. To her horror, she learns that she is a prisoner.

She tells her brother-in-law that her only reason for coming to England was to see him. De Winter is not fooled. He sarcastically acknowledges that her reason for coming is now fulfilled: she is a "guest" in his castle and they can visit together every day. Slyly, de Winter lets Milady know that he is aware of her first husband (Athos), as well as her recent plottings. And when he mentions her branded shoulder, she is ready to kill him – but he warns her not to try, for if she does he will either kill her or send her to the public executioner.

De Winter then calls for his assistant, John Felton, and tells him to guard this wicked woman. He recounts many of the immoral and evil things she has done, and he warns Felton not to be deceived by her. Felton, who is deeply indebted to de Winter for many favors, promises to obey his master's instructions to the letter.

Meanwhile, back in France, the cardinal is wandering around the campgrounds, waiting for Milady's report. By accident, he encounters the four musketeers, who are reading a letter. Richelieu approaches them and engages in a rather guarded political conversation, during which Athos gets the better of the cardinal, who grudgingly leaves.

Commentary

These chapters further reveal the dark and murky depths of Milady's vile nature. For example, other people might have committed some of her immoral acts for the sake of money, but we hear from de Winter that Milady is already wealthy. Milady's desire for de Winter's money is simply another aspect of her enormous greed and lust for power. De Winter finally concludes that her only reason for doing evil is for the sheer pleasure she receives when she is doing it. She can be compared to Shakespeare's Iago (in *Othello*); both Iago and Milady enjoy evil for the sake of evil.

Nonetheless, we should note that in spite of Milady's evil nature, she is treated politely and accommodatingly as a lady should be — rather than being thrown into a dungeon, where she belongs. This politeness is part of the nineteenth century's code of gentlemanly respect for womanhood — even though in this case, Milady's "womanhood" is indelibly corrupt and evil.

In Chapter 51, Athos is rather forward with the cardinal; he suggests that the letter he is reading is from his mistress, and he takes an even more dangerous chance when he says that the letter is not from either of two ladies who have been the cardinal's mistresses. The letter, of course, must be concealed at all costs because it contains the location of the secret whereabouts of Madame Bonacieux — and the cardinal wants this information badly.

CHAPTERS 52–57

Summary

Milady spends her first day in captivity brooding on her fierce hatred for d'Artagnan, Buckingham, and Constance Bonacieux. She wishes them all dead. Her eyes glow with murderous hatred, and she makes elaborate plans for revenge against them. When she finally calms herself, she decides that she should probably study the characters of the men who are guarding her. Foremost, there is John Felton, a seemingly strict disciplinarian.

She pretends to faint, but this ploy doesn't soften Felton's heart, and, to make matters worse, de Winter walks in during the fraudulent fainting fit and tells Felton that Milady's swoon is only her first dramatic performance: she will give many more performances, all demonstrating her considerable talents as an actress. Milady is furious. She grabs a dinner knife – only to discover that it has been blunted. De Winter points out Milady's fury to Felton and again warns him, but this time, Milady notices that Felton seems to have a tiny bit of pity for her.

On the second day, Milady feigns illness, and this time Felton responds sympathetically. He gives her a Catholic missal (a book of masses), and as he does so, she notes that Felton handles the book with distaste, signifying to Milady that he is not a Catholic – he is a Puritan. Thus she pretends to be a victimized Puritan, suffering from Catholic persecution. She summons up all of the pious knowledge that she has accumulated about the Puritans and begins to rant about persecution, martyrdom, and suffering – ideas that are close to a Puritan's heart. She also reads her prayers loudly and fervently, and she sings Puritan hymns like a steadfast victim might. By chance, her voice is so beautiful that Felton is deeply moved and distracted.

On the third day, Milady tries to conceive of a way to make Felton linger in her room. She knows when Felton is coming, so she makes sure that she is ardently praying for the strength to bear her sufferings. In particular, she asks God if the enemy is to be allowed to succeed in his abomination. This show of spiritual earnestness deeply touches young Felton because his religion embraces repentent sinners and elevates martyrs. Milady asks Felton for a favor which he is quick to deny, but he continues to listen to her story, especially when she suggests that de Winter plans to plunge her into shame with Buckingham. Felton can't believe such injustice from de Winter; yet, Milady notices, Felton *is* willing to believe anything derogatory about Buckingham. Felton is surprised to learn that Milady knows Buckingham.

At this point, Milady asks Felton for a knife, promising not to hurt him and promising to return the knife immediately. Felton is convinced that she plans to commit suicide and refuses to give her a knife, but clearly he does believe in her sincerity and goodness. When he leaves, Milady feels that she has Felton within her power.

When de Winter arrives and offers Milady exile or death, she does not choose death. Instead, she begins singing a Puritan hymn so loudly that she can be heard by all the guards.

On the fourth day, young Felton finds Milady playing with a rope made of batiste handkerchiefs. He assumes that she plans to hang herself. She, in turn, accuses him of protecting her body while being an accomplice to the slaughter of her soul. Felton is visibly shaken and tells her that earlier he doubted her sincerity; now, he believes her. Indeed, he is suddenly so fascinated by her that he cannot turn his eyes away from her. As she pleads with him for death, Felton feels the magic of her beauty, her irresistible attraction of sensuality, and her vibrant religious fervor.

Without warning, de Winter enters and breaks Milady's spell. Later, Felton tells Milady that he will return to hear all of her story. She is overjoyed; now she has Felton — "that brainless fanatic" — in her power.

On the fifth day, Milady has her plans prepared; her fictional autobiography is ready. Felton reenters and puts a sharp knife on the table; Milady is further convinced that she has Felton in her power. She tells Felton a long, dramatic story about a nobleman who once tried to seduce her because she was so young and beautiful; she rejected his advances, but he drugged her and then he raped her. Later, she awoke and he stood before her, offering a fortune for her love. She refused and threatened to stab herself. He left, and again she was drugged and raped. Afterward, she still refused — despite threats of more punishment. She vowed that someday she would publish his vile crimes throughout the world. At this point, he threatened to brand her with the mark of a criminal if she murmured a word.

Felton is so moved that he can hardly stand. Milady continues her fictitious story, providing all of the graphic, emotional details, particularly about the sadistic branding. Then, removing just enough of her clothing to entice Felton, Milady reveals the hideous brand, the fleur-de-lis.

When Felton sees the dreadful mark, he is so overcome with passion and fury that he will do anything for her. He demands to know who is responsible for such a crime. Before Milady can answer, though, Felton himself speaks: "Buckingham." He insists on knowing how de Winter is involved. Milady explains that de Winter's brother (her late husband) learned about her past, but married her and promised to kill Buckingham. Yet before he could, he mysteriously died. Buckingham then fabricated stories to her brother-in-law, de Winter, about Milady's shameful past, persuading him that Milady was never in love with de Winter's brother, that she was interested only in the family money. Finishing up, Milady falls dramatically into Felton's arms. He feels the warmth of her breath and the throbbing within her breasts. He has never felt such passion.

De Winter enters, and when Milady threatens to kill herself, he calls her bluff. She takes sudden, drastic measures and cleverly stabs herself in such a superficial way that she draws only a little blood — but it is enough to convince Felton that she is an innocent victim of both de Winter and Buckingham.

Commentary

On the first day of her imprisonment, Milady tries to arouse Felton's sympathy by pretending to faint; the ploy doesn't work. De Winter warns Felton that she will continue to use her immense talents as an actress to gain his sympathy. Later, however, when she puts on a grand performance for Felton, she is so superb that the young, naive Puritan falls for her ruse and also for her beauty and sensuality. Thus, Dumas prepares us for the likelihood that Milady will be able to deceive almost anyone else she wishes to deceive. Clearly, we do not have merely an ordinary villainess here; we have a skillful, talented woman who is the quintessence of evil, possessing the psychological insight to know how to evaluate her victims and how to determine their weak points. She is a magnificent adversary, stunningly powerful and gifted — no match for the naive and sympathetic John Felton.

Note too that Dumas has endowed Milady with all sorts of talents; in addition to her intellectual perceptions, her acting, and her superb deceptions, Milady is endowed with a lovely and piously beautiful voice which converts not only Felton, but also her guards. Yet, never should we forget that at the core of this beautiful body and angelic voice beats the heart of a corrupt and destructive woman. Milady recognizes that a man like Felton can't be tempted by ordinary feminine wiles, and she is astute enough to know that when a man displays extreme piety, he is usually suppressing a secret, passionate nature. Accordingly, she plays on his pity, confessing a multitude of lies about being abducted, drugged, raped and finally branded. Then, playing on his suppressed sensual nature, she reveals to him a lovely naked shoulder, scarred indelibly with a hateful brand.

Her plan is successful: "The enchantress had again taken on the magic power of her beauty and distress, heightened by the irresistible attraction of sensuality mingled with religious fervor." Thus, Dumas, like many modern writers, presents a close correlation between religious fanaticism and sexual passion.

It is to Milady's evil credit that she can seduce Felton's compassion and sympathy so quickly, especially after he has been warned repeatedly about her evil nature—and even after he has seen evidence of her duplicity. However, since Buckingham is known to be something of a "libertine" and a "ladies man," as the Puritans have labeled him, Felton is ready to believe anything about Buckingham; thus, Milady's story of sadistic lust appeals to him. He *wants* to believe wicked things about Buckingham.

The story that Milady tells Felton is filled with stock melodramatic elements, cliches which the innocent Felton readily believes—sleeping potions, drugs, poison, and a virgin deflowered and scarred for life. Ultimately, the dramatic actress finishes her story and pretends to collapse in his arms. Felton gathers up her sensuous body, and apparently this is the first time that he has held such loveliness. He no longer feels pity for her; he worships her.

CHAPTERS 58–59

Summary

De Winter, suspecting that Felton is under Milady's influence, sends him on an errand—away from the castle. That night, Milady hears a tap at the window; it is Felton. He has chartered a boat to take them to France, and he plans to file through the bars on her window and help her escape.

Felton is successful and helps Milady climb down a rope ladder. They board the boat and he tells her that he has to debark at Portsmouth in order to take his revenge on Buckingham before Buckingham leaves for France. Milady is convinced that Felton will be able to dispose of Buckingham; her vengeance will be fulfilled. It is agreed that she will wait for Felton until 10 o'clock before setting sail.

Felton's mind seethes with all of the horrible things he has heard about Buckingham. His strange, maniacal devotion to Milady, together with his fanatical religious notions, make him totally irrational. When he is allowed into Buckingham's office, he pleads for Milady's freedom, but Buckingham absolutely refuses. Crazed, Felton pulls out a dagger and stabs Buckingham. He tries to flee, but he is apprehended by de Winter.

As Buckingham is dying, he learns that Queen Anne's friend, Monsieur de La Porte, is outside; La Porte has a letter from the queen which he reads to the dying Buckingham, assuring Buckingham of Anne's love for him. After Buckingham dies, de Winter questions Felton, who maintains that he killed Buckingham only because of a matter concerning promotions. Then Felton sees the sloop with Milady on it sailing out to sea. Obviously she heard the cannon alerting the nation that something extraordinary had happened, and she surmised that Buckingham was dead. Instantly, she set sail – alone. Felton has been betrayed and abandoned.

Commentary

These two chapters bring to an end the "English episodes" concerning Milady and the puritanical fanatic, Felton, whose religious blindness allowed him to become her dupe. Ironically, the cardinal casually remarked earlier: if all else fails, maybe some fanatic will rid the world of Buckingham. The cardinal was brilliantly prophetic. Dumas has arranged his material so carefully that neither author nor reader wishes to dwell upon the particulars of Felton's religious views; we are content to leave him to his destiny.

Part 5

CHAPTERS 60–63

Summary

After the death of Buckingham, the king of England closes all the ports, but Milady has already escaped, *and* one other ship *also* left. Dumas comments cryptically, "We will later see who was aboard it and how it left."

In France, everyone – including the king – is bored with the siege of La Rochelle. The musketeers, meanwhile, receive a letter from Aramis' ladyfriend, Madame de Chevreuse, with a note that gives freedom to Constance Bonacieux and puts her in their care; the note is signed "Anne."

The king, being bored, needs an escort to Paris, and the four musketeers are among those chosen. In Paris, because they have no pressing duties, they obtain a leave of absence so that they can go to the convent. Once there, d'Artagnan again sees his nemesis, "the man from Meung." As the man rides away, he drops a piece of paper which d'Artagnan retrieves from his servant; on it is written one word, "Armentiers."

Meantime, Milady has also wended her way toward the convent, where she is received as a gracious lady since she has the blessing of the cardinal. However, she senses that the Abbess is not a cardinalist, so she pretends to be a victim of the cardinal (instead of a friend of the cardinal), thereby hoping to gain favor with the Abbess. By chance she learns that another "persecuted person" is at the convent, a woman named Kitty. Milady is anxious to meet this "Kitty," because her own maid Kitty helped d'Artagnan deceive her.

After a brief nap, Milady awakens to discover a beautiful novice standing at her bedside. After they talk, they discover that they are both victims of the cardinal's persecution; Milady, of course, is lying, but she shrewdly questions the other woman and, to her astonishment, she realizes that she is talking to Constance Bonacieux—the very woman she wants killed. Immediately, she ingratiates herself into Constance's confidence, and Constance innocently shares a letter from Madame de Chevreuse. The letter says that d'Artagnan will be arriving for her very soon. At that moment, a man on horseback arrives, asking for "a lady who just came from Boulogne."

The visitor is Count de Rochefort, the cardinal's right-hand man, the person whom d'Artagnan always refers to as "the man from Meung." Milady immediately tells him three important matters: (1) Buckingham is either dead or seriously wounded; (2) she has become a close confidante to Constance Bonacieux, whom the cardinal is searching for; and (3) the four musketeers will be arriving soon. The count is to report immediately to the cardinal, but Milady asks that he leave his chaise, his servant, and his money at her disposal. He is also to instruct the Abbess that Milady is to be allowed to walk in the woods.

Milady then plans her revenge. She pretends that the visitor was her brother, and she convinces Constance Bonacieux that the letter from Madame de Chevreuse is a forgery and that they must flee to a secret cottage that Milady knows about. Suddenly they hear hoofbeats and, leaving Constance seated, Milady peers through the window and sees the musketeers approaching. She tells Constance that it is the cardinal's men and they must escape through the woods. Constance is so paralyzed with fear that she can't move, so Milady pours her a glass of wine, while opening a secret ring and pouring poison into the wine. Then she makes the innocent and trusting Constance drink the wine. Afterward, she flees for her life.

D'Artagnan and the others arrive and find Constance weak and dying. With her last bit of strength, Constance embraces d'Artagnan and tells him that she loves him. As he holds her tenderly in his arms, she is able to remember the name of the woman who gave her the poison. Then she dies, and d'Artagnan "now held only a corpse in his arms." At this moment, de Winter enters, identifies himself and explains that he has been following close behind Milady ever since the death of Buckingham.

D'Artagnan is prostrate with grief, but is comforted by Athos, who tells him to "weep, weep, young heart filled with love, youth, and life!" The other musketeers want to take revenge against Milady immediately, but Athos insists that *he* be in charge because "she is my wife."

Commentary

The king's boredom allows the musketeers the opportunity to accompany him to Paris and, from there, to continue to the convent with the letter from Queen Anne authorizing the release of Constance Bonacieux.

In a romantic novel such as this one, coincidences often play a large part in the plot. Thus, the piece of paper with only the name of a town, "Armentiers," written on it, proves to be a very valuable find because the musketeers feel sure that this is the town where they will be able to find Milady.

At the convent, we again witness Milady's knowledge of psychology and her ability to win the confidence of such different people as the Abbess and Constance Bonacieux. We also see additional proof that Milady is corrupt to the core; she does not even know the young and innocent Constance Bonacieux, but she fiercely desires her death — in order to get even with d'Artagnan. A woman who would sacrifice the life of an innocent victim only to satisfy her own selfish lust for revenge deserves the worst punishment available.

The death of Constance Bonacieux at the very moment that her supposed savior, d'Artagnan, arrives is typical of nineteenth-century melodramatic romanticism. This scene is one that still affects most readers—in spite of its overt use of sentimentalism and contrived timing. The death of this young woman causes Athos, who earlier had been so secretive about his past, to reveal that the scheming, vicious Milady is his wife and that he will take personal charge of punishing her.

CHAPTERS 64–66

Summary

After Athos sends the others to bed, he sends the four servants on four different roads to discover the whereabouts of Milady. Meanwhile, he goes for a walk and begins questioning some late wanderers. Each one of them is so frightened when they hear his question that they cannot speak; they can only point him in a certain direction. Finally, Athos finds an old beggar who is too frightened to accompany him but agrees to do so after Athos gives him a silver coin.

At the small house to which he has been directed, Athos is admitted by a tall, powerful man who shrinks in terror at Athos' request. However, when Athos shows him a piece of paper with the cardinal's signature and seal, the tall man recognizes the seal and agrees to accompany Athos.

Next day, after attending Constance's funeral, Athos investigates the garden and discovers Milady's footsteps. Shortly, Planchet returns with the news that Milady is staying at an inn and that the servants are keeping her under surveillance. That night, they prepare to leave, accompanied by the mysterious tall man, who is wearing a mask and a big red cloak.

Amidst a raging storm, they approach the inn and are led to a cottage, where Athos sees Milady. As she suddenly sees them, Athos breaks through a window, and d'Artagnan comes through the door. Then Porthos, Aramis, de Winter, and the man in the red cloak enter. Athos announces that Milady is to be tried for vile, innumerable crimes—in particular, for poisoning Constance Bonacieux, sending poisoned wine with the intent of killing d'Artagnan, and trying to coerce d'Artagnan to kill Count de Wardes. Then de Winter accuses Milady of corrupting John Felton, of being responsible for the deaths of Buckingham and Felton, and of being responsible for the mysterious death of his own brother – her husband, the first Lord de Winter. Athos then condemns her further because of her deceit in their marriage.

At this point, the executioner – the man in the red cloak – speaks; he reveals her origins and tells how she seduced his brother, a convent priest, to a life of crime. When the crime was discovered, he (as official executioner) had to brand his own brother. Milady escaped, he says, by seducing the jailer's son. She also helped the priest to escape. The executioner managed to track her down and brand her. He himself had to serve his missing brother's remaining prison term. Later, after Milady abandoned the priest for Athos (Count de La Fère), the priest surrendered, then hanged himself.

Athos asks each of the men for a verdict. Each one of them asks for the death penalty. Milady is carried to the edge of a river where she is tied hand and foot, and once again her crimes are recounted as she begs for her life. The executioner takes her across the river, and in the boat she frees her feet and tries to escape, but she cannot get up. The executioner cuts off her head, wraps her body and head in his cloak and dumps them in the river, crying out loudly, "God's justice be done."

Commentary

These chapters bring to an end the horrible injustices of Milady – Lady de Winter. As in most nineteenth-century novels, justice triumphs and evil is destroyed. But not before Dumas introduces one last mystery. In Chapter 64, he creates a wonderful sense of suspense when he has everyone who is quizzed by Athos quail before him, afraid to tell him where a certain person lives. As we discover later, Athos is looking for an executioner, and most simple and superstitious people fear such a man – even though he is only doing his job. It is poetic justice that Milady loses her life at the hands of an "official" executioner – especially since he suffered so terribly as a result of her evil conniving.

Moviemakers often revel in filming this final scene, where the climax of raging emotions and passions parallel the raging storm outside, suggesting the furious storms within the protagonists.

When the various men gather to denounce Milady's numerous and infamous sins, the list is truly impressive – a list that chills most people, but note that Milady feels that she is being treated unfairly. Even though she herself has just killed Constance Bonacieux, a young, innocent woman, Milady pleads that she herself is "too young" to die. Milady's death fits the crimes that she committed: her head, the source of all her conniving, is severed from her body and both pieces are thrown into the river. With her death, justice has been done, and the novel can now draw rapidly to an end.

CONCLUSION & EPILOGUE

Summary

The French king is overjoyed to learn that Buckingham is dead; in addition, he is finally able to return to the siege. On the way, he and the musketeers stop at an inn where "the man from Meung" appears and tells d'Artagnan that he is under arrest. He identifies himself as Count de Rochefort, Cardinal Richelieu's agent. D'Artagnan's three comrades will not allow him to be arrested; they promise to deliver him to the cardinal at the appointed time.

Later, the cardinal tells d'Artagnan that he is accused of conspiring with enemies of France, intercepting state secrets, and attempting to thwart his general's plans. D'Artagnan defies the cardinal to name his accuser. He states that his accuser is a woman branded by French justice, a bigamist who poisoned her second husband, tried to poison d'Artagnan, poisoned Constance Bonacieux, and was guilty of many other crimes.

When d'Artagnan finishes the tangled story of Milady's web of crimes, including her being sentenced to death, a shudder runs through the cardinal's body. Still, though, he thinks that d'Artagnan should be tried. It is then that d'Artagnan shows the cardinal the carte blanche "paper of protection" which the cardinal himself gave to the wicked Milady, stating, "The bearer of this letter has acted under my orders and for the good of the State. Richelieu."

The cardinal pauses, sits and writes. D'Artagnan wonders if it is his death sentence. It is not. The cardinal has written out a commission for "someone" to serve as a first lieutenant in the musketeers; d'Artagnan can fill in any name he chooses. The cardinal reminds d'Artagnan, however, that the opportunity is given to *him*. D'Artagnan first offers the commission to Athos, but Athos refuses it because he has inherited some money. Then Porthos turns it down because his mistress has inherited a fortune. Aramis refuses it because he is finally entering a monastery. Thus, d'Artagnan has to accept the commission.

The novel ends with d'Artagnan's fighting three duels with Count de Rochefort. Then Cardinal Richelieu orders them to become friends. To seal the friendship, Count de Rochefort makes Planchet a sergeant in the guards.

Commentary

After only a short time in Paris, our young Gascon has evolved, as did Monsieur de Tréville, from being a country boy to being a power to be reckoned with in the King's Musketeers. He is now a friend of the cardinal and also a defender of the queen. The other musketeers are happy and living their own individual lives. Here, as in most nineteenth-century novels, all's well that ends well.

CRITICAL ESSAY

THE THREE MUSKETEERS AS FILM

Dumas' novel has appealed to filmmakers of the world ever since the beginning of commercial cinema. In this country alone, there have been many different films based on Dumas' masterpiece. Some versions remain reasonably faithful to the novel, while other versions use some of Dumas' general plot outlines, or the characters, or the era, and then stray variously from the novel itself.

One of the early films which was based on *The Three Musketeers* starred Douglas Fairbanks, probably the most famous "swashbuckling" actor of the silent film industry. In fact, this movie almost singlehandedly set the tone for the Douglas Fairbanks–style of acting which has, in one way or another, influenced later productions and acting styles for similar movies. That is, Fairbanks was filmed swinging from chandeliers, brandishing swords, perilously crossing deep, craggy ravines, fighting against insurmountable odds, and performing other improbable feats of bravado and bravery. The film is 186 minutes long, an extremely long movie for a silent film; usually silent films lasted 60 to 90 minutes.

Another film version of *The Three Musketeers* was released in 1933. This cinematic treatment of the novel contained sound, but was a rather brief, truncated version of the story. The director terribly mis-cast a youthful John Wayne as one of the musketeers.

The 1935 version of the novel starred Walter Abel, an actor known for his dignity and reserve; not surprisingly, he made d'Artagnan one of the most boring swordsmen ever. Not recommended.

The 1939 *Three Musketeers* film starring the Ritz Brothers—Al, Jimmy, and Harry—used Dumas' title as a vehicle for the rich comic talents of the three zany brothers. Very little attention was given to Dumas' plot; Don Ameche (a recent Oscar winner) was cast as d'Artagnan, but he failed to make the role memorable. The movie should be seen only for the antics of the three Ritz Brothers as the three irrepressible musketeers.

Recently, there have been efforts to create sequels for Dumas' original novel. Among them, *The Fifth Musketeer* has been given a screen treatment, as well as a movie featuring d'Artagnan as an aging swordsman, still gallant and dashing, but now more of a Don Quixote figure.

Of all the movie versions, however, most movie critics agree that the best were released in 1949 and 1974. The 1949 *Three Musketeers* featured an all-star cast of MGM notables. Director George Sidney cast Gene Kelly as d'Artagnan; Van Heflin as Athos; June Allison as Constance; Lana Turner as Milady; Vincent Price as Richelieu; and Angela Lansbury as Queen Anne. This film version, unlike the 1974 production by Richard Lester, is unusually faithful to Dumas' novel. Consider, for instance, the fidelity of the film to the novel in the following key scenes.

Scene 1. As d'Artagnan departs from home, he is cleanly and neatly dressed, although he is a peasant lad; he receives gifts from his father and departs on a very comic-looking horse. In contrast, this same scene in the 1974 Richard Lester film, starring Michael York as d'Artagnan, shows the hero dressed in dirty, ragged clothes, conducting himself rather basely and departing on a perfectly acceptable-looking horse.

Scene 2. D'Artagnan's arrival in Meung is memorable because of his impetuous attack on "the man from Meung"; d'Artagnan attempts to duel with the stranger, but is defeated, beaten and robbed. In Lester's film, the duel scene and the fighting are played wholly for comedy.

Scene 3. D'Artagnan's arrival in Paris and his admittance to Tré-ville's house shows him overhearing Athos, Porthos, and Aramis being reprimanded for dueling in a tavern. This scene is omitted in Lester's film.

Scene 4. D'Artagnan catches sight of "the man from Meung," runs after him, bumps into Athos and agrees to a 12 o'clock duel; he knocks Porthos down, revealing a half-golden (instead of an entirely golden) shoulder belt, and agrees to a 1 o'clock duel; then he enrages the usually quiet Aramis and agrees to a 2 o'clock duel. In the Lester film, there are so many extraneous things happening that one loses all sense of any individuality among the three musketeers.

Scene 5. During d'Artagnan's duel with Athos, while the other two musketeers wait their turn, the duel is interrupted by the appearance of the cardinal's men, who arrive to arrest them; d'Artagnan sides with the musketeers and thereby becomes an unofficial "fourth" musketeer.

While this is a rather short scene in the novel, it is usually presented in the movies in the grand tradition of the great dueling scenes established by Douglas Fairbanks. In the Sidney film, it is a continuous, running scene, marvelously orchestrated and brilliantly choreographed. Each of the duelists is individualized with the ultimate and final attention focused on the magnificent performance by Gene Kelly as d'Artagnan. In his heyday, Kelly was one of the finest dancers on the silver screen, and this particular scene emphasizes his masterful ability to move and dance.

The three musketeers finally retire to the background and function merely as an appreciative audience as this fantastic peasant lad from Gascony deliciously combats with finesse and, at times, with humor – always in control of the situation. The entire scene functions as a complete cinematic unit.

In contrast, the Lester version is filmed as though it were a back street brawl, with no continuity of camera work; each short, jerky shot has little or no relation to the next short, jerky shot. Instead of long, lyric passages of classic dueling, Lester has his swordsmen doing karate chops, kicking, gouging, jumping, bludgeoning with rakes and poles, and other such related nonsense. There is absolutely no sense of d'Artagnan's being a superior swordsman.

Scene 6. After Tréville reprimands the four men and they are summoned to an audience with the king, the scene of them marching through the elegant throne room and up to the king is a classic scene which is often used or recreated for advertising purposes. Curiously, this entire scene is deleted from the Lester film and replaced with odd doings of street people and gratuitous acrobats, circus-like activities, and other visual diversions inserted to create a sense of "atmosphere."

From this point on, the Sidney film varies only slightly from the novel. However, note that Constance Bonacieux becomes Monsieur Bonacieux's adopted *daughter;* thus the love affair between her and d'Artagnan was more acceptable to the moral code of the late '40s than d'Artagnan's having an affair with his landlord's *wife.* In the Lester movie, the young and beautiful Constance is played by an aging but voluptuous Raquel Welch, who is immediately attracted to d'Artagnan; the two are in bed within minutes of meeting one another.

From this point on in the Lester film, there is little similarity to Dumas' novel. The Sidney film, however, continues to follow Dumas' novel almost scene for scene. Admittedly, there are some "adjustments"—such as placing Milady under the guard of Constance, instead of introducing a new character (John Felton in the novel), and later, there is a serious divergence from the novel when Milady goes to her death proud and defiant, rather than pleading and conniving, as she does in the novel.

In conclusion, the 1949 movie is a very close rendering of Dumas' literary masterpiece, whereas the 1974 movie uses the basic plotline of the novel, but creates an entirely different sort of finished product.

SUGGESTED ESSAY QUESTIONS

1. The three musketeers—Athos, Porthos, and Aramis—are often thought of collectively, yet each of them is a unique individual. Discuss their individual differences and show how these differences are reflected in their choice of servants—for example, in Athos' Grimaud, Porthos' Mousqueton, and Aramis' Bazin.

2. Write on the relationship between adventure, intrigue, love, and mystery throughout the novel.

3. Discuss the significant occurrences (events, happenings, adventures, coincidences) which allow d'Artagnan, a simple young eighteen-year-old boy, to become a twenty-one-year-old man of position and power.

4. How does Cardinal Richelieu affect d'Artagnan's rise to fame more than do d'Artagnan's friends?

5. Discuss the correlation between the duke of Buckingham's love for Queen Anne and d'Artagnan's love for Constance Bonacieux.

6. Discuss Milady as the pure essence, or quintessence, of evil.

SELECTED BIBLIOGRAPHY

BASSAN, FERNANDE. *Alexandre Dumas, pere, et la Comedie-Francaise.* Paris: Lettres Modernes, 1972.

BELL, A. CRAIG. *Alexandre Dumas, a Biography and Study.* London. Cassell, 1950.

COOK, MERCER. *Five French Negro Authors.* Washington, D.C.: Associated Publishers, 1943.

GORMAN, HERBERT SHERMAN. *The Incredible Marquis, Alexandre Dumas.* New York: Rinehart, 1929.

HEMMINGS, FREDERICK WILLIAM JOHN. *The King of Romance: A Portrait of Alexandre Dumas.* London, 1929.

LUCAS-DUBRETON, JEAN. *La Vie d'Alexandre Dumas, pere.* Paris: J. Lucas-Dubreton, 1916.

MAUROIS, ANDRE. *Alexandre Dumas: A Great Life in Brief.* New York: Knopf, 1955.

MUNRO, DOUGLAS. *Alexandre Dumas, pere.* New York: Garland, 1981.

PARIGOT, HIPPOLYTE LOUIS. *Alexandre Dumas, pere.* Paris, 1902.

REED, FRANK WILD. *Alexandre Dumas, Benefactor.* New York: Colophon, 1935.

Ross, Michael. *Alexandre Dumas*. London: Newton Abbot, 1981.

Schop, Claude. *Alexandre Dumas: Genius of Life*. New York: Franklin Watts, 1988.

Simon, G. M. *Histoire d'une Collaboration*. Paris, 1919.

Stowe, Richard. *Alexandre Dumas*. New York: Twayne, 1976.

Thompson, John A. *Alexandre Dumas, pere, and the Spanish Romance Drama*. Louisiana State University Press, 1938.

NOTES